PAIR
AND
COMPARE

Developing Reading Skills

Geoff Barton
and Mary Bousted

D1337456

Collins Educational

An imprint of HarperCollinsPublishers

Published by Collins Educational
An imprint of HarperCollins*Publishers*
77–85 Fulham Palace Road, London W6 8JB

© HarperCollins*Publishers* 1994

First published 1994
Reprinted 1994, 1995, 1996

ISBN 0 00 3230422

Design by Carla Turchini
Cover design by Wendi Watson
Cover illustration: *Senecio* by Paul Klee, 1922/Bridgeman Art Library

Printed and bound in Great Britain by Scotprint Ltd, Musselburgh

Commissioning editor: Domenica de Rosa
Editor: Rebecca Lloyd
Production: James Graves

CONTENTS

INTRODUCTION

Pair and Compare is an anthology of lively reading materials for use in the classroom. As we were compiling the book, we were told by teachers that what they wanted was a greater variety of texts – non-literary as well as literary materials, contemporary sources alongside pre-twentieth century selections, whole texts and extracts.

We have grouped the material around themes and genres, and our chief purpose is to provide a combative mix of texts in order to provoke discussion, debate and analysis. You will find that texts relating to similar subjects are placed side by side, but that their authors often take radically opposed views. This should lead to some lively classwork.

READING SKILLS

We are also keen that the anthology should help teachers to focus on specific aspects of reading, hence our subtitle. We do not see the reading process as a narrowly mechanistic one, in which pupils tick off one skill and move on to the next, but we do recognize that teachers need to focus increasingly precisely on what pupils need to practise. The skills we are concerned with in *Pair and Compare* are:

1   Developing personal response
2   Reading for meaning
3   Reading aloud
4   Seeking information
5   Identifying key points
6   Summarising
7   Scanning/skimming
8   Distinguishing fact from fiction/detecting bias
9   Analysing language
10   Studying genre

Our list of reading skills is not narrowly tied to the National Curriculum for English. Instead, it is a list of the skills and experiences which we believe pupils need to develop in order to become confident and effective readers. To support the teacher we have ensured that our activities focus on specific skills. We have not included 'reading for pleasure' as a reading skill because we see it as fundamental to our entire selection.

USING THE BOOK

Pair and Compare is arranged in nine units, each covering a particular theme. Within each unit, texts are placed in pairs, or in larger groups, and occasionally one text stands alone. After each text, you will find short 'After Reading' questions which aim to take pupils *back into* the text and deepen their understanding. Sometimes there are also 'Before Reading' questions. Following each group of texts is a 'Compare' section containing longer 'Discussion' and 'Assignment' questions. These aim to help pupils think more carefully about the language and, finally, to take them *beyond* the text – to examine wider issues and principles.

We have aimed to ensure a variety of responses to texts, encouraging pupils to discuss what they have read in groups, to analyse, think and rethink, and write about their conclusions.

PRE-TWENTIETH CENTURY LITERATURE

We have sought pieces of earlier writing which really work in class, making them rub shoulders with contemporary extracts on similar themes. Our belief here is that the *content* will provide pupils with a way into the text – an initial point of comparison – before they move on to look more closely at the writer's *language*. We think pre-twentieth century literature is important not because it was written in the past, but because it has something distinctive to say – and this has been our chief criterion for selection.

DIFFERENTIATION

This is a book for pupils of all abilities. We have included accessible texts alongside very demanding ones, and aimed to provide activities and approaches which will support pupils working at all levels. The suggested activities always provide for a wide degree of differentiation, and we suggest that you guide pupils to the assignment most appropriate to their interests and abilities.

CONCLUSION

We hope that you will find *Pair and Compare 1* a source of lively and stimulating lesson materials, and that the layout proves attractive and easy to use. The companion book for Key Stage 4, *Pair and Compare 2*, provides a further range of texts and resources to provoke debate and analysis with GSCE students.

GEOFF BARTON
MARY BOUSTED

EARLY DAYS

Many adults talk about their childhood as a kind of golden age, when life was exciting, entertaining and happy. Perhaps it was like that. Or perhaps they forget the embarrassments, humiliations and sufferings.
- *How do you remember your early days?*
- *What have been the most significant experiences in your life so far?*
- *How do you think your childhood compares with the experiences of people in the past?*

HOLIDAYS PAST

■ The following poem and novel extract describe childhoods in the first half of this century. The children are going on holiday.

READING SKILLS

Developing personal response

Reading aloud

Beside the seaside

Green Shutters, shut your shutters! Windyridge,
Let winds unnoticed whistle round your hill!
High Dormers, draw your curtains! Slam the door,
And pack the family in the Morris eight.
Lock up the garage. Put her in reverse,
Back out with care, now, forward, off – away!
The richer people living farther out
O'ertake us in their Rovers. We, in turn,
Pass poorer families hurrying on foot
Towards the station. Very soon the town
Will echo to the groan of empty trams
And sweetshops advertise Ice Cream in vain.

Solihull, Headingley and Golders Green,
Preston and Swindon, Manchester and Leeds,
Braintree and Bocking, hear the sea! the sea!
The smack of breakers upon windy rocks,
Spray blowing backwards from their curling walls
Of green translucent water. England leaves
Her centre for her tide-line. Father's toes,
Though now encased in coloured socks and shoes
And pressing the accelerator hard,

Ache for the feel of sand and little shrimps
To tickle in between them. Mother vows
To be more patient with the family;
Just for its sake she will be young again.
And, at that moment, Jennifer is sick
(Over-excitement must have brought it on,
The hurried breakfast and the early start)
And Michael's rather pale, and as for Anne...
"Please stop a moment, Hubert, anywhere."

So evening sunlight shows us Sandy Cover
The same as last year and the year before.
Still on the brick front of the Baptist Church
SIX-THIRTY. PREACHER: – *Mr. Pentecost* –
All visitors are welcomed. Still the quartz
Glitters along the tops of garden walls.
Those macrocarpa still survive the gales
They must have had last winter. Still the shops
Remain unaltered on the Esplanade –
The Circulating Library, the Stores,
Jill's Pantry, Cynthia's Ditty Box (Antiques),
Trecarrow (Maps and Souvenirs and Guides).
Still on the terrace of the big hotel
Pale pink hydrangeas turn a rusty brown
Where sea winds catch them, and yet do not die.

The bumpy lane between the tamarisks,
The escallonia hedge, and still it's there –
Our lodging-house, ten minutes from the shore.
Still unprepared to make a picnic lunch
Except by notice on the previous day.
Still nowhere for the children when it's wet
Except that smelly, overcrowded lounge.
And still no garage for the motor-car.
Still on the bedroom wall, the list of rules:
Don't waste the water. It is pumped by hand.
Don't throw old blades into the W.C.
Don't keep the bathroom long and don't be late
For meals and don't hang swim-suits out on sills
(A line has been provided at the back).
Don't empty children's sand-shoes in the hall.
Don't this, Don't that. Ah, still the same, the same
As it was last year and the year before –
But rather more expensive, now, of course.
"Anne, Jennifer and Michael – run along
Down to the sands and find yourselves some friends
While Dad and I unpack." The sea! The sea!

JOHN BETJEMAN

AFTER READING

1 What sort of holiday are this family going to have?

2 Pick out three words or expressions which indicate that the poem is set in the past.

Five on Finniston Farm

'Phew!' said Julian, mopping his wet forehead. 'What a day! Let's go and live at the Equator – it would be cool compared to this!'

He stood leaning on his bicycle, out of breath with a long steep ride up a hill. Dick grinned at him. 'You're out of training, Ju!' he said. 'Let's sit down for a bit and look at the view. We're pretty high up!'

They leaned their bicycles against a nearby gate and sat down, their backs against the lower bars. Below them spread the Dorset countryside, shimmering in the heat of the day, the distance almost lost in a blue haze. A small breeze came wandering round, and Julian sighed in relief.

'I'd never have come on this biking trip if I'd guessed it was going to be as hot as this!' he said. 'Good thing Anne didn't come – she'd have given up the first day.'

'George wouldn't have minded,' said Dick. 'She's game enough for anything'.

'Good old Georgina,' said Julian, shutting his eyes. 'I'll be glad to see the girls again. Fun to be on our own, of course – but things always seem to happen when the four of us are together.'

'*Five*, you mean,' said Dick, tipping his hat over his eyes. 'Don't forget old Timmy. What a dog! Never knew one that had such a wet lick as Tim. I say – won't it be fun to meet them all! Don't let's forget the time, Julian. Hey, wake up, ass! If we go to sleep now, we'll not be in time to meet the girls' bus.'

Julian was almost asleep. Dick looked at him and laughed. Then he looked at his watch, and did a little calculating. It was half past two.

'Let's see now – Anne and George will be on the bus that stops at Finniston Church at five past three', he thought. 'Finniston is about a mile away, down this hill. I'll give Julian fifteen minutes to have a nap – and hope to goodness I don't fall asleep myself!'

He felt his own eyes closing after a minute, and got up at once to walk about. The two girls and Tim *must* be met, because they would have suitcases with them, which the boys planned to wheel along on their bicycles.

The five were going to stay at a place called Finniston Farm, set on a hill above the little village of Finniston. None of them had been there before, nor even heard of it. It had all come about because George's mother had heard from an old school friend, who had told her that she was taking paying guests at her farm-house – and had asked her to recommend visitors to her. George had promptly said she would like to go there with her cousins in the summer holidays.

'Hope it's a decent place!' thought Dick, gazing down into the valley where corn-fields waved in the little breeze. 'Anyway, we shall only be there for two weeks – and it *will* be fun to be together again.'

He looked at his watch. Time to go! He gave Julian a push. 'Hey, wake up!'

''Nother ten minutes,' muttered Julian, trying to turn over, as if he were in bed. He rolled against the gate-bars and fell on to the hard damp earth below. He sat up in surprise. 'Gosh – I thought I was in bed!' he said. 'My word, I could have gone on sleeping for hours.'

'Well, it's time to go and meet the bus,' said Dick. 'I've had to walk about all the time you were asleep, I was afraid I'd go off myself. Come on, Julian – we really must go!'

They rode down the hill, going cautiously round the sharp corners, remembering how many times they had met herds of cows, wide farm carts, tractors and the like, on their way through this great farming county. Ah – there was the village, at the bottom of the hill. It looked old and peaceful and half-asleep.

'Thank goodness it sells ginger-beer and ice-creams!' said Dick, seeing a small shop with a big sign in the window. 'I feel as if I want to hang out my tongue, like Timmy does, I'm so thirsty!'

'Let's find the church and the bus-stop,' said Julian. 'I saw a spire as we rode down the hill, but it disappeared when we got near the bottom.'

'There's the bus!' said Dick, as he heard the noise of wheels rumbling along in the distance. 'Look, here it comes. We'll follow it.'

'There's Anne in it – and George, look!' shouted Julian. 'We're here exactly on time! Whoo-hoo, George!'

The bus came to a stop by the old church, and out jumped Anne and George, each with a suitcase – and out leapt old Timmy too, his tongue hanging down, very glad to be out of the hot, jerky, smelly bus.

'There are the boys!' shouted George, and waved wildly as the bus went off again. 'Julian! Dick! I'm so glad you're here to meet us!'

The two boys rode up, and jumped off their bikes, while Timmy leapt round them, barking madly. They thumped the girls on their backs, and grinned at them. 'Just the same old sixpences!' said Dick. 'You've got a spot on your chin, George, and why on *earth* have you tied your hair into a pony-tail, Anne?'

'You're not very polite, Dick,' said George, bumping him with her suitcase. 'I can't think why Anne and I looked forward so much to seeing you again. Here, take my suitcase – haven't you any manners?'

'Plenty,' said Dick, and grabbed the case. 'I just can't get over Anne's new hair-do. I don't like it, Anne – do you, Ju? Pony-tail! A donkey-tail would suit you better, Anne!'

'It's all right – it's just because the back of my neck was so hot,' said Anne, shaking her hair free in a hurry. She hated her brothers to find fault with her. Julian gave her arm a squeeze.

'Nice to see you both,' he said. 'What about some ginger-beer and ice-cream? There's a shop over there that sells them. And I've a sudden longing for nice juicy plums!'

'You haven't said a *word* to Timmy yet,' said George, half-offended. 'He's been trotting round you and licking your hands – and he's so dreadfully hot and thirsty!'

'Shake paws, Tim,' said Dick, and Timmy politely put up his right paw. He shook hands with Julian too and then promptly went mad, careering about and almost knocking over a small boy on a bicycle.

'Come on, Tim – want an ice-cream?' said Dick, laying his hand on the big dog's head. 'Hark at him panting, George – I bet he wishes he could unzip his hairy coat and take it off! Don't you, Tim?'

'Woof!' said Tim, and slapped his tail against Dick's bare legs.

ENID BLYTON

1 How can you tell that this adventure is set in the past? Look at characters, behaviour, description and language.

2 What differences do you notice between the portrayal of the boys and the girls?

COMPARE

Discussion

1 In pairs, prepare a reading of the poem. What tone should you use – should it be funny or sad; that of a teacher, child or parent? Practise reading aloud in different styles.

In small groups of five or six, prepare a reading of the story. Work out who will play which part, and practise different voices. Again, think about your tone – could the passage be read in a humorous way? One person will need to read the narrator's words. Which reading was the most successful and why?

2 With your partner, discuss and note down the similarities and differences between John Betjeman's and the Five's holidays. Which holiday is more like your own? Which type of holiday would you prefer?

3 Both texts deal with adults' views of childhood. Think of five words which describe the images of childhood portrayed in each piece of writing.

4 How could you update the poem or story for modern readers? What changes would you make to the presentation of characters, places and language?

Assignments

1 Write a 'reading autobiography' in which you look back at the books which have most influenced you during your life. Look at the opening of this personal essay written by Laura Gladwin, aged thirteen.

"The earliest book I remember is called *In the Night Kitchen* by Maurice Sendak. I would probably have had it read to me around the age of four or five. The storyline is not particularly pleasant: a boy named Mickey falls into the 'Night Kitchen' and is made into a Mickey Cake by some oversized bakers with sinister smiles on their faces. Mickey manages to escape and promptly falls into a huge bottle of milk, claiming, 'I'm in the milk and the milk's in me'. I was always a bit disturbed by the book, but for some reason I was fascinated by it."

Like Laura Gladwin, aim to get a balance between telling the story and describing your memories of each book.

2 Write your own children's adventure story in the style of *Five on Finniston Farm*. Start by inventing a new gang of children as your characters, and set the story in the past.

WORKING CHILDHOODS

■ In contrast to the portrayal of happy early days given by John Betjeman and Enid Blyton, read now about some real-life and fictional experiences of children in the last century who were sent to work. William Hutton was only seven when he started work.

Working in the Silk-mill

My days of play were now drawing to an end. The Silk-mill was proposed. One of the clerks remarked to the person who took me there, that the offer was needless, I was too young. However, the offer was made; and, as hands were wanted, in the infant state of this work, I was accepted. It was found, upon trial, that nature had not given me length sufficient to reach the engine, for, out of three hundred persons employed in the mill, I was by far the least and the youngest.

It is happy for man that invention supplies the place of want. The superintendents wisely thought, if they could lengthen one end it would affect both. A pair of high pattens were therefore fabricated, and tied fast about my feet, to make them steady companions. They were clumsy companions, which I dragged about one year, and with pleasure delivered up.

I had now to rise at five every morning during seven years; submit to the cane whenever convenient to the master; be the constant companion of the most rude and vulgar of the human race, never taught by nature, nor ever wishing to be taught. A lad, let his mind be in what state it would, must be as impudent as they, or be hunted down. I could not consider this place in any other light than that of a complete bear-garden....

Entering the gates of the mill, at noon, a strong wind blew off my hat, which rolled before me into the Derwent. I could have gone swifter than the hat, but knew I should acquire a velocity that would have run me into the river, which, being deep, I had lost my life. In distress, I travelled by its side, the whole length of the building, but it continued just out of my reach. I mourned its loss the whole afternoon, as well as dreaded the consequence.

My master informed the chief Governor, who ordered him to take me to a hatter, and purchase another. I was asked whether I would have a plain band, or one with a silver tassel? What child refuses finery? I chose the latter, and became the envy of the mill.

Christmas holidays were attended with snow, followed by a sharp frost. A thaw came on, in the afternoon of the 27th, but in the night the ground was again caught by a frost, which glazed the streets. I did not awake, the next morning, till daylight seemed to appear. I rose in tears, for fear of punishment, and went to my father's bed-side, to ask what was o'clock? 'He believed six;' I darted out in agonies, and from the bottom of Full street, to the top of Silkmill lane, not 200 yards, I fell nine times! Observing no lights in the mill, I knew it was an early hour, and that the reflection of the snow had deceived me. Returning, it struck two. As I now went with care, I fell but twice....

In pouring some bobbins out of one box into another, the cogs of an engine caught the box in my hand. The works in all the five rooms began to thunder, crack and break to pieces; a universal cry of 'Stop mills' ensued; all the violent powers of nature operated within me. With the strength of a madman I wrenched the box from the wheel; but, alas, the mischief was done. I durst not shew my face, nor retreat to dinner till every soul was gone. Pity in distress was not found within those walls.

WILLIAM HUTTON

AFTER READING

1 Pick out three surprising or disturbing facts about William Hutton's life at work.

2 How does the writer gain our sympathy for what he describes?

■ Very young children were ideal for sweeping chimneys, since they were small enough to climb up and down them.

The Chimney Sweeper

When my mother died I was very young,
And my father sold me while yet my tongue
Could scarcely cry "'weep! 'weep! 'weep!'
So your chimneys I sweep, & in soot I sleep.

There's little Tom Dacre, who cried when his head,
That curl'd like a lamb's back, was shav'd: so I said
'Hush, Tom! never mind it, for when your head's bare
'You know that the soot cannot soil your white hair.'

And so he was quiet, & that very night,
As Tom was a-sleeping, he had such a sight!
That thousands of sweepers, Dick, Joe, Ned, & Jack,
Were all of them lock'd up in coffins of black.

And by came an Angel who had a bright key,
And he open'd the coffins & set them all free;
Then down a green plain leaping, laughing, they run,
And wash in a river, and shine in the Sun.

Then naked & white, all their bags left behind,
They rise upon clouds and sport in the wind;
And the Angel told Tom, if he'd be a good boy,
He'd have God for his father, & never want joy.

And so Tom awoke; and we rose in the dark,
And got with our bags & our brushes to work.
Tho' the morning was cold, Tom was happy & warm;
So if all do their duty they need not fear harm.

WILLIAM BLAKE

HARDENING THE FLESH

No one knows the cruelty which a boy has to undergo in learning. The flesh must be hardened. This is done by rubbing it, chiefly on the elbows and knees with the strongest brine, as that got from a pork-shop, close by a hot fire. You must stand over them with a cane, or coax them by a promise of a halfpenny, etc. if they will stand a few more rubs.

At first they will come back from their work with their arms and knees streaming with blood, and the knees looking as if the caps had been pulled off. Then they must be rubbed with brine again, and perhaps go off at once to another chimney. In some boys I have found that the skin does not harden for years.

AFTER READING

1 What is the message of the poem?

2 What facts do you learn from the poem about the life of child sweeps?

■ The following testimony was given by the master sweep Ruff of Nottingham to the Children's Employment Commission of 1863.

The best age for teaching boys is about six. That is thought a nice trainable age. But I have known two at least of my neighbours' children begin at the age of five. I once saw a child only 4½ years in the market-place in his sooty clothes and with his scraper in his hand...he began when he was four.

AFTER READING

1 What is the purpose of the brine?

2 Which word best describes the speaker's tone – concerned, neutral, factual, upset, angry, indignant?

The Water Babies

Once upon a time there was a little chimney-sweep, and his name was Tom. That is a short name, and you have heard it before, so you will not have much trouble in remembering it. He lived in a great town in the North country, where there were plenty of chimneys to sweep, and plenty of money for Tom to earn and his master to spend. He could not read nor write, and did not care to do either; and he never washed himself, for there was no water up the court where he lived. He had never been taught to say his prayers. He never had heard of God, or of Christ, except in words which you never have heard, and which it would have been well if he had never heard. He cried half his time, and laughed the other half. He cried when he had to climb the dark flues, rubbing his poor knees and elbows raw; and when the soot got into his eyes, which it did every day in the week; and when his master beat him, which he did every day in the week; and when he had not enough to eat, which happened every day in the week likewise. And he laughed the other half of the day, when he was tossing halfpennies with the other boys, or playing leapfrog over the posts, or bowling stones at the horses' legs as they trotted by, which last was excellent fun, when there was a wall at hand behind which to hide. As for chimney-sweeping, and being hungry, and being beaten, he took all that for the way of the world, like the rain and snow and thunder, and stood manfully with his back to it till it was over, as his old donkey did to a hail-

storm; and then shook his ears and was as jolly as ever; and thought of the fine times coming, when he would be a man, and a master sweep, and sit in the public-house with a quart of beer and a long pipe, and play cards for silver money, and wear velveteens and ankle-jacks, and keep a white bull-dog with one grey ear, and carry her puppies in his pocket, just like a man. And he would have apprentices, one, two, three, if he could. How he would bully them, and knock them about, just as his master did to him; and make them carry home the soot sacks, while he rode before them on his donkey, with a pipe in his mouth and a flower in his button-hole, like a king at the head of his army. Yes, there were good times coming; and, when his master let him have a pull at the leavings of his beer, Tom was the jolliest boy in the whole town.

CHARLES KINGSLEY

AFTER READING

1 Think of three words which describe Tom's character.

2 How can you tell that this extract is a fictional rather than a factual account? Look closely at the writer's use of language.

■ The Water Boy in this folksong was the boy who brought water to the convicts working on the roads.

Water Boy

Water Boy where are you hiding;
If you don't-a come
Gwine tell-a yoh Mammy.

There ain't no hammer
That's on-a this mountain
That ring-a like mine, boys,
That ring-a like mine.

Done bus' this rock, boys,
From hyeh to Macon
All th' way to th' jail, boys,
Yes back to th' jail.

You Jack-o-Di'monds,
Yo Jack-o-Di'monds
Ah know yeh of old, boys,
Yes, know yeh of ol'.

You robbed my pocket,
Yes robba my pocket
Done a-robba my pocket,
Of silver an gol'.

ANON

AFTER READING

1 What signs are there that this extract was intended to be sung rather than read?

2 How, in a sentence, would you summarise the meaning of the song?

COMPARE

Discussion

1 With your partner, discuss which of the extracts you found most interesting and why.

2 In small groups, discuss which of these words could be applied to each extract – factual, brutal, descriptive, emotional, disturbing. List the words in order of their suitability for each extract. Try to find examples from the texts to support your decisions.

3 Choose two or three of the extracts and discuss how the writers gain our sympathy for what they describe.

Assignments

1 Write a diary entry, or the opening of an autobiography, as if you were a child in the harsh world of Victorian Britain. See the Wider Reading list at the end of this unit for other books which might help you with this assignment.

2 Using a tape recorder, interview a relative about his or her childhood. Write a transcript of the interview, then write a paragraph highlighting the main differences between the conditions of your interviewee's childhood and your own.

3 Write a personal essay about a moment that changed your life. It could be a memory of personal achievement or of sadness. Establish the background to the event (when? where? who?) and then describe what happened (how? why?).

4 Make a poster showing the different facts you have learnt about children from these extracts.

TWO MEMOIRS

■ Two writers recall their own childhoods in the Welsh and English countryside.

READING SKILLS
Identifying key points
Analysing language

A Welsh Childhood

We had a small front garden with a little wooden gate and a slate path. There was a lilac tree on the left with banks of snow-in-summer growing underneath it. On the right was a fuchsia hedge and my mother tried to grow dahlias but the sheep used to jump down the wall from the mountain and eat them. I never used the gate in the evenings. There was a toehold in the wall and with one bound you were free and up on *ffrith*. With my whole body I can remember that toehold.

I went to the National School on the coast road and, since Penmaenmawr slopes as it does, my first classroom was half underground. In the winter it was warmed by an open stove and we did our sums on wood-framed slates using slated pencils which, licked and held in a certain way, made the sort of noise that drives some people mad –

like a long fingernail scratching a nylon stocking. Certain of my friends, having discovered the power of this noise, would slide the last part of the road to school down the slate-lined gutters with a granite chipping under foot.

I had enemies too. There was a boy called Robert who lived in Penmaenan (all our enemies lived in Penmaenan, which was out of bounds except for raiding parties) who had thick glasses and a chronic dribble, and used to chase me round the playground. He caught me and kissed me one day, and I was reprimanded by the headmaster, who said he would never have expected such a thing of me. I have never recovered from the injustice of this and I hope Robert has had a rotten life. Then there was a little English boy whose name I never knew, who didn't even attempt to fraternize with the natives but played trains all by himself, going *choo choo* and working his elbows like pistons. The badder boys jeered at him in the playground and he once made a response so dignified and so touching that I wept. I can't remember what it was, but the memory still brings tears to my eyes. I dare say today I should want to smack him.

As time went by our teacher, G.O. Jones, taught us, among other things, to write properly, with a pen. This involved penholders and nibs and wipers and ink monitors whose duty it was to refill the inkwells on each desk, which must have been quite tricky since most of us used them as receptacles for the cod-liver oil capsules and iron pills which a caring authority deemed necessary for our health. G.O. had been gassed in the First World War and as a result he spat a bit as he spoke, and our exercise books came up in moisture bubbles when he stood beside us. He, too, had trouble with Robert whose mother used to burst in roaring when her boy had been quite correctly caned. G.O. said she was a *blackguard* and I admired this sophisticated choice of words, although I wouldn't have cared to cross her myself. There were several women like this around, gypsy-like and intimidating, and quite unlike the majority who wore black straw hats and gloves to Chapel and high-necked, black garments and never swore.

The most remarkable of the foul-mouthed ladies lived near us on the top road in a cottage which stood – or rather was falling down – on its own. She was called Bonny Mary and she had a brother called John Tom who was mad. He spoke to no one but himself and would stride, stick in hand, along the top road jumping, at intervals, into the air, glaring and gesturing and concerned only with some private irritating matter. Many people used to take their constitutionals along the top road: the nuns from the local convent and Father Hugh from the Franciscan friary. Bonny Mary had a son and daughter too and they all slept, as far as we could tell, on heaps of sacks and old newspapers. There was very little furniture to be seen through the open door. I don't think her children went to school. I never saw them there. She was considered to be a witch.

There were many witches in Wales. The nastiest was the Gwrach y Rhibyn who was about ten feet tall and whose breath killed you. Then there were two sisters who kept an inn with a bad reputation near Llandudno. They used to turn themselves into cats and steal the guests' gold and watches, which I would have thought would be easier to accomplish if you retained your human form, your fingers and pockets – but it wouldn't make such a good story. They came to the usual end. One intrepid traveller stayed awake, whacked the prowling cat on the leg with a stick and, lo and behold, next morning one of the ladies pronounced herself incommoded and unable to come down to breakfast. When she did appear she had a shocking limp.

Two other sisters who lived in the foothills of Snowdonia were themselves bothered by a cat-witch. They had had a very plain serving maid who fell in love with the fiancé of one of them. Perhaps this made her dreamy, for she was sacked for incompetence and thrown out to live in a cave and sustain herself as best she could on stolen turnips from the fields. Shortly afterwards the sister exhibited fearful scratches on their faces and it was decided that the aggrieved maid had transformed herself into a cat and devoted herself to ruining their beauty. I myself think it more likely that both sisters were in love with the fiancé and the scratches were the result of sibling rivalry and strife. Clearly, however, it would have been more dignified and acceptable to the family if they could put the blame on the cat. Cats, being such beautiful creatures, sufficient unto themselves, have always aroused envy in human beings. Too often people resort to kicking the cat.

School became more onerous as the scholarship approached. My first teacher, Miss Roberts, a dear feathery old person, had let me draw fairies when I should have been doing sums and I never did get the hang of the things, so I was made to go for private lessons to Mr Pugh, an ex-schoolteacher who lived with his wife in a cold, clean house with a ticking clock. These lessons were hell – as much, I imagine, for the unfortunate Pugh as they were for me – since I was incapable even of short division and simply couldn't see the point. He asked, one day, as I seemed not to be concentrating, if I was frightened of him and I explained that it was just that I'd rather be playing with the Joneses on the clinker pile outside the laundry. Clinkers were what was left of the coke which fed the boilers, and it has only just occurred to me to wonder why they were dumped on the roadside and not taken away. I don't remember the pile ever getting any smaller.

This laundry also stood on the top road and the washing was hung to dry in the field behind. We thought it was height of wit to take in live shrews (which we took off the cats) to frighten the laundry girls who all, so the local wisdom went, had perfect complexions from working in a steamy atmosphere. Jack Laundry drove the van and his wife, Jenny Laundry, made perfect chutney. Chutney was an important aspect of life in Penmaenmawr.

The Joneses – there were six of them, but the little ones didn't count much in those days – had evolved a complex and fast-moving game with a ball and the clinker heap. People were stationed at various points and heights on the clinkers, the ball went round and you took it from there. It seems perverse to have been playing on the detritus from the laundry boilers with the Snowdon range beginning behind us, but it was nearer home and our mothers could call us in for tea without having to trudge up Moelfre. The Jones children had evolved a noise – a war whoop – by which we could recognize and discover each other up on the hills. It was quite difficult to do, starting low in the throat and rising, but was effective once mastered.

I now feel nostalgic for that school by the sea. We were taught calmly and authoritatively what our teachers deemed it necessary for us to know, and often in the afternoon G.O. would tell us stories – not read out from books, but the living legends of the locality. The oral tradition was still strong then, and I can think of no better start in life for a person who is going to end up as a writer. I hated sums, and the warm milk we had to drink at playtime (we used to try and shake the little bottle until the milk turned into butter – something the Celts have been doing since the dawn of history, not in bottles, naturally, but in skins and churns and anything which would be agitated), and Robert, who took to throwing stones at me (I still bear the scars), and being caned, which didn't happen often but was painful when it did (you were advised by your peers to spit in the hand which was going to take the punishment and lay two hairs from your head crosswise over the spit, but it didn't work), but I liked the darkening winter afternoons with the iron stove glowing and the endless stories. I think I was fortunate.

ALICE THOMAS ELLIS

AFTER READING

1 Using the headings 'People' and 'Places,' quickly note down the main events you recall from Alice Thomas Ellis's memoir.

2 Do you think she had a happy childhood? Discuss in pairs.

■ Dirk Bogarde recalls his childhood with his sister, his cousin, Flora, and Lally, the housemaid.

SNOWFALL

I was just lying there: it was very warm and safe-feeling. I knew it was still dark because there was no ragged line of light round the curtains and I could hear Flora snoring, or moaning, in her bed. My sister was probably curled up with her head under the quilt. She always slept like that, only this time I couldn't see her because it was dark. But if I turned my head and looked through Flora's room I could see the orange glimmer round Lally's bedroom door, and that was her getting up. So, worse luck, as soon as she'd got on her pinafore, tidied up her hair and shaken her alarm clock (she always did this to see if it was still working even though she could hear it ticking, but it was just something she did anyway, to be quite certain), I knew the door would creak open and she'd come through the rooms and tell us to start waking up, quick sharp, and that another day was starting and there was this or that to do if we wanted any breakfast. I knew it by heart, I suppose.

'Time to wake up! Lots to do before breakfast!' she said. (You see?) And then she saw I was awake. 'There's a surprise for you all outside ... better get your skates on before it goes.' She was holding her candle high so that shadows danced across the bumpy plaster walls and made the beams black and wavery. She had her indoor shoes in her other hand, so as not to wake us up, except that she had already woken us. 'What is it?' I said and sat up, and felt the cold slither right down my back.

'Been a fall of snow overnight. Still as still ... but it won't lie. Best put on your woolly stockings from the top drawer. It's a very cold morning.' And then she opened the door to the stairs and went rustling down while I reached for the box of Swan Vestas by the candlestick.

When we all got down to the kitchen, and after I'd looked to see if all was well with the Weekend (which it was), the light was goldeny brown from the paraffin lamp and the candle, and the range was crackling and Lally was pumping up the Primus ... the other one had a singing kettle on it – well, not exactly singing, but sighing really. It was still dark outside, but if you pressed hard against the cold glass, and shaded your face against the lamplight with your hands, you could see, as clear as clear, that everything outside was white.

'It'll be light in a few minutes, near eight o'clock, and as soon as it is, and as soon as you've had a good hot drink, taken your Virol, got on your Wellingtons, then it's off with you all to do a bit of wooding for the kindling pile while I get the toast and porridge ready. And I want no arguments!' She looked very serious, one hand on hip, bread knife in the other. I mean, it was sticking up! You couldn't argue with her.

'What's for breakfast?' I said, pouring milk from the milk-can into a jug.

'Tea, toast and six eggs! And out of my way, I've a busy day today.' She wagged the knife at me, 'Toot de sweet, now!'

My sister came clumping down the stairs doing up her snake-belt. It was her most favourite thing, and she'd pinched it from me, but I had a second, so it didn't worry me really. But she wore it even with her good flannel skirt from school. Not just her shorts, like she did in summer. 'You said it was snowing!' she grumbled. 'That's what you said,' and she began to pull up her school socks which were woollen and awful-looking things. Wrinkled grey worms.

'It *was* snowing! I said there had been a light fall, if I'm right – and no one try to correct me. It's stopped now, and you'll come to no harm and I reckon you won't see a polar bear, no more a penguin, where you are going. And please set the sugar on the table. Flora! Flora! Come along now, do. Breakfast is about to begin. Flora! Do I have to bang a gong?'

'She wouldn't know what a gong was,' I said. 'And the wood will be all snowy, all the kindling and everything.'

'So what's the use?' said my sister huffing about looking for the Tate and Lyle on the dresser.

'The use is that I need the kindling, so shake the snow off – don't dare bring it into the house and make all the rest sodden!'

'But there is masses of kindling, we got piles yesterday!'

'And you'll get piles today! Or else my name is not Ellen Jane...'

My sister looked at me across the table and made a twisty face, and we both began to snort a bit, and Lally suddenly got a bit red in the face, the way she did when she thought we were being rotten behind her back but she didn't know.

'What's all the sniggering in aid of, pray? That range uses the kindling like straw, and there's the sitting-room fire to be lit to air the room for your parents, and I want the copper lit this afternoon...' She started to slice up the big cottage loaf for toast. You could see she was being a bit huffy about the sniggering part because she suddenly said, quite crossly, 'Your grammar! Upon my word! What would your father say? "Good Grammar Teached Here Gooder Up The Stairs." That's what. "Is" and "are", remember. And now out of my way.'

But you could see she was fretting, and then Flora came down the stairs looking pretty silly in a raggedy woollen red and yellow tartan hat which she said was her Tam o'Shanter. And it had a stupid pom-pom on the top which wobbled about. She looked really jolly funny, wandering about the kitchen pulling the hat this way and that.

Lally took the kettle off the Primus and poured it into the big brown teapot. 'I want no more private laughter from you two,' she said, 'and no *quibbling!* No quibbling at all. Wooding after your tea and Virol, breakfast *after.* Then you all get washed and do teeth.' And looking at Flora she said, in her Polite-to-Guest voice, 'Flora dear, what are you about? Not in the house dear, not in the house.' And then she set the jar of Virol on a saucer and put three spoons round it, like the spokes in a wheel.

Flora pulled out her chair and sat down. She wasn't a bit afraid of Lally, mostly because Lally was always so terribly sweet to her. When she spoke to her, anyway.

'It's against the cold,' she said firmly. I thought she was very brave. 'My father says that our heads are like yon chimney. All the heat in your body just rises up and goes out of the top of your head. And he was a soldier in the war and he should know.'

'Well...quite right. But your head will be nice and warm in my kitchen, now I've got it all cosy and comfy for you, so I'll be obliged if you'd remove your hat at my table, please. You'll lose nothing through the top of your head except your brains. Off with it, please, Madam Caledonia!'

So Lally won. Well, she nearly always did. So the silly Tam o'Shanter came off and we drank our tea, had the Virol and licked the spoons.

DIRK BOGARDE

AFTER READING

1 What are the main events of this extract?

2 How does the writer use language to create a sense of enthusiasm?

COMPARE

Discussion

1 Make a list of the similarities and differences between the two writers' childhoods – their backgrounds, memories, and attitudes.

2 Do you think the writers idealize their childhoods, or are their descriptions realistic? Is one extract more idealistic than the other? Find evidence to support your ideas.

3 Both writers describe their childhoods, but their styles are quite different. Use these headings to try to define the differences:
- dialogue
- length of sentences
- links from one idea to the next
- vocabulary
- narrator's voice

Assignments

1 How would you begin your own autobiography? What if a publisher told you that the most boring place to start describing your life is at the beginning? Where would you start instead – at the present, working backwards? Or by focusing on a key moment? Have a go at writing the first chapter of your autobiography.

2 Research the childhood of a famous person you are interested in, using an encyclopaedia, or dictionary of biography. Write a brief account of his or her early days, saying in particular what signs you can detect of the person he or she would become.

3 Choose one moment from your childhood and write about it in two styles. First write a brief (150-word) factual account, giving the main details. Then write it in a more descriptive way, adding dialogue and atmosphere. Which proved easier or more enjoyable to write?

WHEN WE WERE VERY YOUNG ═══════

■ What are your memories of life at nursery or primary school? See how far they resemble Joyce Grenfell's version.

For best effect, listen to Joyce Grenfell performing her monologue, or read it aloud yourself.

Developing personal response

Reading aloud

Sing-Song Time

Children, we've had our run around the classroom, and now it's time to start our day's work. We're going to have a sing-song together, and Miss Boulting is going to play for us, so come and settle down over here, please.

Kenny, why haven't you taken your coat off?

No, it isn't time to go home yet, Kenny! You've only just come.

You'd rather go home? Bad luck.

No, you can't go, not quite yet.

Kenny, you've only been here about ten minutes. Come and sit on the floor next to Susan.

You like Susan.

No, Susan, I don't think he wants to sit on your lap.

No, I thought he didn't.

Kenny! We don't want to see your tongue, thank you.

No, not even ▾ little bit of it. Put it back, please.

All of it.

And give your jacket to Caroline, I'm sure she'll hang it up for you.

Thank you, Caroline.

Who is that whistling?

Sidney, you know we never whistle indoors. You can whistle in the garden, but we never whistle indoors.

Yes, I know you have just whistled indoors, but don't do it anymore.

And don't punch Jacqueline.

I'm sure she didn't say she liked you punching her, did you Jacqueline?

Well, I don't think it's a good idea, so we won't have any more punching.

He is rather a disruptive element in our midst, Miss Boulting, but he does try to belong more than he used to, so we are encouraged, bless his heart.

Let's be *kind* to each other today, shall we? We are going to learn some more of the Drum Marching Song we began yesterday.

Who remembers how it starts?

No, David, it doesn't begin 'Twinkle, Twinkle Little Star'. That's another song.

Yes, I know you know it, but we aren't going to sing it now.

No. Not today.

And not tomorrow.

I don't know when.

We are going to sing our Drum Marching Song now.

Edgar and Neville, why are you standing on those chairs?

You can see into the fish-tank perfectly well from the floor. Get down, please.

No, Neville, you can't hold a fish in your hand.

Because fishes don't like being held in people's hands. They don't like coming out of the water, you see. Their home is in the water.

Well, they do have to come out of the water when we eat them, but these aren't *eating* fishes. These are *friend* fishes. It's Phyllis and Fred. We wouldn't want to eat Phyllis and Fred.

No, Sidney, you wouldn't.

I don't think they'd be better than sausages.

Come back, please. You don't have to go and see Phyllis and Fred. You know them perfectly well.

I don't know what they are doing behind the weeds, Sidney. Just having a nice friendly game, I expect.

Neville, you tell us how the Drum Marching Song begins.

Yes! That's right.

'Rum tum tum, says the big bass drum'. Well remembered, Neville.

When we know the song well we're going to march to the Drum Song. But today we'll just stand and sing it; so, everybody ready?

'Rum tum tum, says the big bass drum.'

Just a minute, Miss Boulting.

Where is your drum, Kenny? No, not on your head. It's in front, isn't it, on a make-believe string round your neck.

Sidney, I heard what you said. You know it isn't 'Rum tum tummy'.

It may be funnier, but it isn't right.

Yes, it is a funny joke. Let's get the laughter over, please.

Finished?

Now then. Ready?

Thank you, Miss Boulting.

'Rum tum tummy...'

Yes, I made a mistake. It was silly, of me, wasn't it? Yes, very silly.

Sh– sh–. It wasn't as silly as all that.

I think we'll go on to the next bit perhaps...

Miss Boulting...

'Rooti-toot-toot, says the...

Who says 'Rooti-toot-toot', David?

No, David, not 'Twinkle Twinkle'.

Yes, Lavinia, the *'Cheerful* Flute'.

And what is a flute?

No, Dicky, it isn't an orange.

It isn't a banana.

It isn't an apple.

It isn't FRUIT, it's FLUTE.

FLUTE.

And what is a flute?

Yes, Lavinia, it's in a band. It's a musical instrument in a band. And how do we play it?

No, we don't kick it and bash it about, Sidney.

Now think.

We *blow* it.

Yes, Edgar, we *blow* it, and the music comes out of it. It's a musical instrument, and we *blow* down it.

Rachel, don't blow at Timmy.

And Timmy, don't blow back.

I'm sorry she blew you a very wet one. But don't blow a wet one back.

Now use your hankies, and wipe each other down, both of you. I'm sure you're both sorry.

No, Kenny, it isn't time to go home yet.

Shirleen, why are you taking your skirt off?

I'm sure Mummy wants you to keep it nice and clean, but you won't get it dirty from singing, you know.

Yes, it is very pretty.

Yes, and it's got little doggies all over it. Little blue and little pink doggies. Put it on again, please. Yes, your panties are pretty; *and* your vest.

But pull down your skirt now.

George. Remember what I asked you not to do?

Well, then...

'Rooti-toot-toot, says the cheerful flute.'

Rest.

Sidney, you're whistling again. And if you are going to whistle you must learn to do it properly. You don't just draw in your breath like that, you have to blow in and out.

It's no good saying you bet I can't whistle, because I can. I've been able to whistle for a very long time, but I'm not going to do it now. But I can.

I don't know why I compete with him, Miss Boulting. I really shouldn't.

Let's start our Drum Marching Song from the very beginning, shall we?

What did you say, Miss Boulting?

Already! So it is. Oh, good. And here is Mrs Western with our milk and biscuits.

Get into a nice straight line by the trolley, please.

No, Kenny, it isn't time to go home yet. There is still an hour and a half to go...

JOYCE GRENFELL

AFTER READING

1 Write down your impressions of the teacher who delivers this monologue – her age, looks, voice, attitude to children and thoughts as she is speaking.

Discussion

1 Choose three key moments from the monologue and improvise or discuss the thoughts that are going on in the teacher's mind.

2 In pairs, think of some constructive advice to give to this teacher.

3 Working in groups of four, present the monologue as a piece of drama, paying particular attention to the way the teacher attempts to control the children. Perform your version to the rest of the class, and discuss any points where you disagree about interpretation.

Assignments

1 Choose one of the children and write the monologue from his or her point of view, giving the thoughts that occur to the child during sing-song time.

2 Choose a real event from your own days at primary school and write about it, either in a personal essay, or in a monologue or diary form.

WIDER READING

Childhood Reminiscences

Penelope Hughes-Hallet, *Childhood: A Collins Anthology* is especially recommended; Roald Dahl, *Boy* and *Going Solo*; Paul Zindel, *The Pigman and Me*; Alice Thomas Ellis, *A Welsh Childhood*; Flora Thompson, *Larkrise to Candleford*; John Mortimer, *Clinging to the Wreckage*. Accounts of North American slavery are gathered together in Margaret Busby's brilliant anthology, *Daughters of Africa*.

Novels about childhood

Charles Dickens, *David Copperfield*; Charlotte Brontë, *Jane Eyre*; Robert Westall, *The Scarecrows*; Jane Gardam, *God on the Rocks*; Stan Barstow, *Joby*; Nina Bawden, *Carrie's War*.

1 Write about two of the texts you have most enjoyed, recommending their qualities to a new reader.

2 Look critically at some books written especially for people of your age. Write an essay discussing how young people are portrayed. Are boys and girls treated differently?

DUMB ANIMALS

Human beings have a complex relationship with animals. We would never eat our pet dog, yet many of us will eat farm animals.
- *Why do people object to hunting when animals hunt each other and can hunt people?*
- *How many of us oppose vivisection and yet take medicines that have been tested on animals?*

THE HUNTER AND THE HUNTED

■ These two passages describe a hunter – the panther. In the poem the panther is hunting another animal.

READING SKILLS

Identifying key points and ideas

Reading for meaning

AFTER READING

1 Make a list of the words in the poem that describe the panther's movements. In pairs, discuss what sort of picture the poet is painting of the panther.

2 What are the differences between the hunter (the panther) and the victim (the tapir)?

Living Cloud

Creeping through the Amazon forest,
Vines and undergrowth part before his mighty head.
Looking like a stormcloud in the jungle.
Water glints in the moonlight.
He has come to the greatest river on earth.
He dares not cross it because of cannibal fish known
      as piranhas.
His glossy shoulders go up and down like pistons.
Gracefully he leaps onto a low branch of a breadfruit tree,
Waiting for some unlucky creature to wander below the
      tree that conceals him.
His four black feet brandishing claws, gripping
      the branch.
Suddenly the blunder buss of the Amazon forest comes.
He announces himself with a squealing whistle.
The panther's muscles tense.
Then he leaps upon the unsuspecting tapir.
Roaring he pounces on the tapir, claws ripping,
      jaws biting.
The tapir gives one last squeal.
The panther drags the carcase to the river where
      he can drink with his meal.

STEPHEN BELL

■ In this extract a fourteen-year-old school-boy, Billy, is hunted by a panther which has escaped from a travelling circus, and has killed sheep and people on the moors around a northern town.

THE NATURE OF THE BEAST

I must have been less than a mile away from Kirkby Haverston when I began to get this feeling. I'd started listening for something without really noticing that that was what I was doing. And then the hair began to creep on the back of my neck, and I did notice.

There was nothing to hear, and yet I was hearing something. I didn't slow down. I didn't stop and look round. I didn't walk any faster at first – because walking faster would have been like admitting there was something there. And now the crunch of my boots was like interference. The sounds I was listening for were so small and faint, and I couldn't tell where they were coming from.

It was like trying to stretch your ears to hear further. And then, on the rise of the road ahead, something moved against those millions of stars, like a silhouette blocking them out for less than a second.

The Beast wasn't behind me. It was ahead, between me and the village, and behind me was only five miles of empty road and all the darkness of Aggerton Moss.

I stopped dead and stared into the dark, but I couldn't see anything now, except all the humps of grass and all the tussocks either side of the road looked like things crouching. I wanted to unwrap my air-rifle, but I daren't make a sound.

There were no trees, nowhere to run to. And no sound of a car. I didn't know how fast panthers can run, but I knew it would be a bloody sight faster than me.

Then I heard the sound, softer than a real sound almost. Padding. It was hard to hear because my heart was beating that loud. Coming towards me, down the dark slope of the road.

I kept having this really stupid thought about a black cat in a coal cellar. It's our art teacher's joke. He draws a square on the blackboard and says "What's that a picture of?"

Groan. "A black cat in a coal cellar, Sir."

There's no way I can describe how scared I was.

And suddenly I couldn't stand still any longer. I dropped my bag and made a run for it, tearing the dustbin liner off my air-rifle. Maybe I yelled. I can't remember. I can only remember running – not back the way I'd come, but sideways, into the marsh and peat of Aggerton Moss.

I was squelching and splashing and stumbling about in the dark, trying to pull the lid off a tin of slugs in my pocket, and trying not to drop the air-rifle into the water.

And, behind me, I could hear it, softly, almost dainty, padding along on big cat feet. Even without looking, I could see the way it would spring from tussock to tussock, jump peaty streams I was wading through and half sinking up to my knees in, with the icy water making me want to scream.

And the Beast wasn't even trying. It was just loping softly along.

I didn't just think I might die – I knew I was going to. I'd never see Dad again.

I could hardly breathe, and it felt like someone had started pole-axing me in the ribs. And part of me couldn't believe any of this was happening at all.

"Chunder! Dad! Dad!" this voice was screaming. But it stopped after a while.

Then Aggerton Moss grabbed me by the legs. I'd run smack into a moss pool – like quicksand, only it's a deep hole full of sphagnum moss and wet peat. I tried to heave my legs out, sucking and squelching, round the edge. Hardly moving at all, but just moving a bit, and the coldness... The freezing coldness.

I stopped. I'd gone down up to my thighs nearly. I didn't want to run any more – I just wanted to be dead and warm. And I couldn't run any more. Struggling was only making me sink deeper.

Then the panther came. Hardly running. It stopped at the edge of the moss pool and growled. I saw a flash of white teeth, a cloud of breath.

It sprang – more like playful than full stretch. A small jump.

I fired the air-rifle. Its bang was loud and stupid, like a kid bursting a paper bag.

The Beast was in the middle of the moss pool. It roared. But it didn't come any closer. It was sinking! Roaring, and plunging up and down, trying to drag itself out!

I could smell its breath. Warm. Beast. No. I can't describe it.

I cranked my air-rifle and fired it again – I don't know if I hit it or not, but it didn't like the noise at any rate! And it's plunging and growling and thrashing its tail. Coming closer, but sinking! Sinking! Sinking!

"Sink! Sink, yer devil!" I was screaming, I managed to crank up one more shot, then I started chucking slugs at its head. The whole pool's wallowing and I've gone down a bit further, but I'm still here and it can't bloody reach me! And all I know was – the more it thrashed, the more it would sink.

So I'm yelling at it, and trying to load up and crank, and wanging slugs and handfuls of freezing muddy moss!

And it's roaring and snarling – and stuck! Bloody stuck!

I tried to back out, sitting down nearly and falling backwards, and still chucking slugs, and beating at the water with my air-rifle, until I could grab some grass and pull, slow as hell, slow as dying, slowly, slowly, until the weight's off my legs and I can pull myself clear!

It's like a bloody miracle! I'm dancing up and down, and yelling and howling, and shooting slug after slug almost leisurely like. I can't believe it! And this cat screaming almost – horrible it is.

Snarling! Screaming! Thrashing about! Going on forever.

Then suddenly it's quiet. No. I mean the roaring stops. And I've stopped yelling and shooting. There's just sucking and splashing noises, and the Beast's going to die. It's going down, death in its silence, death in its struggling. The black water's shining, and the terrible earth smell of it all churned up – stinking it is. And the Beast doesn't look like a cat any more – it looks like a water monster. Humpy back, its head bony with all its fur wet. Bubbles – hardly seeing them as much as hearing them.

And then there's only the silence of Aggerton Moss. Stars. Ripples fading on the moss pool. The orangey glow of Haverston. Silence.

I didn't kill the Beast – Aggerton Moss did.

I was sick. My legs crumpled and I spewed up, retching and retching, until I just couldn't any more. And I was crying my head off.

You ask anyone at *The Cocks* what state I was in when I crawled through the pub door.

I'd lost one of my boots in the moss. I was soaked to the bone. I think now I would have died if it hadn't been for those two cars. Oh – they didn't stop. They never saw us. But I saw the headlights and I crawled in that direction. It wasn't like the films when people get up and stride away. I crawled until I got to the road. I was still clutching my air-rifle, using it like a stick and a lever.

I hardly remember getting to the village at all. Just retching up nothing but burning spit, and shaking until it felt like all my bones were going to jump out of their sockets or break.

I hardly even remember getting to the pub. Just lights. And people all talking, and someone pulling all my clothes off and shoving me in a bath. Blankets. Drinking hot whisky or brandy. And spewing up again.

Then Chunder being there, and me in a bed, croaking, "Don't turn the light off!" The Beast was dead, but I didn't want to be in the dark.
And crying. I remember Chunder's rough old hand trying to stroke me, and me crying. Very quietly. Because I was alive.

Because the Beast was dead.

JANNI HOWKER

AFTER READING

1 Working in pairs, make a list of the signs that Billy gets that he is being hunted by the panther. In a second column, choose one word to describe what Billy is feeling at that moment. Set out your list like this:

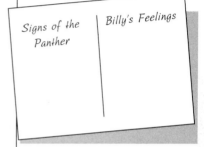

Signs of the Panther	Billy's Feelings

2 Later, Billy cries because the panther is dead. What do you think he might be crying for?

COMPARE

Discussion

1 In the poem, the tapir dies. In the extract, the panther dies. Discuss which death is more disturbing and why.

2 Discuss whether you think that wild animals like the panther should be kept in zoos or in circuses.

3 The panthers' appearance and the way they move are descibed in both the poem and the novel extract. Using this information, write your own description of a panther and present it to the class.

Assignments

1 Imagine that you are the panther. Rewrite the hunt of the tapir, OR the hunt of Billy, from the panther's point of view.

2 The tapir is unaware that it is going to die; Billy is terrified because he knows that the panther is hunting him. Write an essay in which you say which of the two descriptions of the hunts you found to be more effective and why.

MY FAMILY AND OTHER ANIMALS ══════

■ This story is set in Corfu. The narrator, Gerry, is an animal addict. Unfortunately, the rest of his family do not share his enthusiasm.

The World in a Wall

The crumbling wall that surrounded the sunken garden alongside the house was a rich hunting ground for me. It was an ancient brick wall that had been plastered over, but now this outer skin was green with moss, bulging and sagging with the damp of many winters. The whole surface was an intricate map of cracks, some several inches wide, others as fine as hairs. Here and there large pieces had dropped off and revealed the rows of rose-pink bricks lying beneath like ribs. There was a whole landscape on this wall if you peered closely enough to see it; the roofs of a hundred tiny toadstools, red, yellow, and brown, showed in patches like villages on the damper portions; mountains of bottle-green moss grew in tuffets so symmetrical that they might have been planted and trimmed; forests of small ferns sprouted from cracks in the shady places, drooping languidly like little green fountains. The top of the wall was a desert land, too dry for anything except a few rust-red mosses to live in it, too hot for anything except sun-bathing by the dragon-flies. At the base of the wall grew a mass of plants, cyclamen, crocus, asphodel, thrusting their leaves among the piles of broken and chipped roof-tiles that lay there. This whole strip was guarded by a labyrinth of blackberry hung, in season, with fruit that was plump and juicy and black as ebony.

The inhabitants of the wall were a mixed lot, and they were divided into day and night workers, the hunters and the hunted. At night the hunters were the toads that lived among the brambles, and the geckos, pale, translucent with bulging eyes, that lived in the cracks higher up the wall. Their prey was the population of stupid, absent-minded crane-flies that zoomed and barged their way among the leaves; moths of all sizes and shapes, moths striped, tessellated, checked, spotted, and blotched, that fluttered in soft clouds along the withered plaster; the beetles, rotund and neatly clad as business men, hurrying with portly efficiency about their night's work. When the last glow-worm had dragged his frosty emerald lantern to bed over the hills of moss, and the sun rose, the wall was taken over by the next set of inhabitants. Here it was more important to differentiate between the prey and the predators, for everything seemed to feed indiscriminately off everything else. Thus the hunting wasps searched out caterpillars and spiders; the spiders hunted for flies; the dragon-flies, big, brittle, and hunting-pink, fed off the spiders and the flies; and the swift, lithe, and multi-coloured wall lizards fed off everything.

But the shyest and most self-effacing of the wall community were the most dangerous; you hardly ever saw one unless you looked for it, and yet there must have been several hundred living in the cracks of the wall. Slide a knife-blade carefully under a piece of the loose plaster and lever it gently away from the brick, and there, crouching beneath it, would be a little black scorpion an inch long, looking as though he were made out of polished chocolate. They were weird-looking things, with their flattened, oval bodies, their neat, crooked legs, the enormous crab-like claws, bulbous and neatly jointed as armour, and the tail like a string of brown beads ending in a sting like a rose-thorn. The scorpion would lie there quite quietly as you examined him, only raising his tail in an almost apologetic gesture of warning if you breathed too hard on him. If you kept him in the sun too long he would simply turn his back on you and walk away, and then slide slowly but firmly under another section of plaster.

I grew very fond of these scorpions. I found them to be pleasant, unassuming creatures with, on the whole, the most charming habits. Provided you did nothing silly or clumsy (like putting your hand on one) the scorpions treated you with respect, their one desire being to get away and hide as quickly as possible. They must have found me rather a trial, for I was always ripping sections of the plaster away so that I could watch them, or capturing them and making them walk about in jam-jars so that I could see the way their feet moved. By means of my sudden and unexpected assaults on the wall I discovered quite a bit about the scorpions. I found that they would eat bluebottles (though how they caught them was a mystery I never solved), grass-hoppers, moths, and lacewing flies. Several times I found them eating each other, a habit I found most distressing in a creatures otherwise so impeccable.

By crouching under the wall at night with a torch, I managed to catch some brief glimpses of the scorpions' wonderful courtship dances. I saw them standing, claws clasped, their bodies raised to the skies, their tales lovingly entwined; I saw them waltzing slowly in circles among the moss cushions, claw in claw. But my view of these performances was all too short, for almost as I switched on the torch the partners would stop, pause for a moment, and then, seeing that I was not going to extinguish the light, they would turn round and walk firmly away, claw in claw, side by side. They were definitely beasts that believed in keeping themselves *to* themselves. If I could have kept a colony in captivity I would probably have been able to see the whole of the courtship, but the family had forbidden scorpions in the house, despite my arguments in favour of them.

The one day I found a fat female scorpion in the wall, wearing what at first glance appeared to be a pale fawn fur coat. Closer inspection proved that this strange garment was made up of a mass of tiny babies clinging to the mother's back. I was enraptured by this family, and I made up my mind to smuggle them into the house and up to my bedroom so that I might keep them and watch them grow up. With infinite care I manoeuvered the mother and family into a matchbox, and then hurried to the villa. It was rather unfortunate that just as I entered the door lunch should be served; however, I placed the matchbox carefully on the mantelpiece in the drawing-room, so that the scorpions should get plenty of air, and made my way to the dining-room and joined the family for the meal. Dawdling over my food, feeding Roger surreptitiously under the table and listening to the family arguing, I completely forgot about my exciting new captures. At last Larry, having finished, fetched the cigarettes from the drawing-room, and lying back in his chair he put one in his mouth and picked up the matchbox he had brought. Oblivious of my impending doom I watched him interestedly as, still talking glibly, he opened the matchbox.

Now I maintain to this day that the female scoprion meant no harm. She was agitated and a trifle annoyed at being shut up in a matchbox for so long, and so she seized the first opportunity to escape. She hoisted herself out of the box with great rapidity, her babies clinging on desperately, and scuttled on to the back of Larry's hand. There, not quite certain what to do next, she paused, her sting curved up at the ready. Larry, feeling the movement of her claws, glanced down to see what it was, and from that moment things got increasingly confused.

He uttered a roar of fright that made Lugaretzia drop a plate and brought Roger out from beneath the table, barking wildly. With a flick of his hand he sent the unfortunate scorpion flying down the table, and she landed midway between Margo and Leslie, scattering babies like confetti as she thumped on the cloth. Thoroughly enraged at this treatment, the creature sped towards Leslie, her sting quivering with emotion. Leslie leapt to his feet, overturning his chair, and flicked out desperately with his napkin, sending the scorpion rolling across the cloth towards Margo, who promptly let out a scream that any railway engine would have been proud to produce. Mother, completely bewildered by this sudden and rapid change from peace to chaos, put on her glasses and peered down the table to see what was causing the pandemonium, and at that moment Margo, in a vain attempt to stop the scorpion's advance, hurled a glass of water at it. The shower missed the animal completely, but successfully drenched Mother, who, not being able to stand cold water, promptly lost her breath and sat gasping at the end of the table, unable even to protest. The scorpion had now gone to ground under Leslie's plate, while her babies swarmed wildly all over the table. Roger, mystified by the panic, but determined to do his share, ran round and round the room, barking hysterically.

'It's that bloody boy again...' bellowed Larry.

'Look out! Look out! They're coming!' screamed Margo.

'All we need is a book,' roared Leslie; 'don't panic, hit 'em with a book.'

'What on earth's the *matter* with you all?' Mother kept imploring, mopping her glasses.

'It's that bloody boy...he'll kill the lot of us....Look at the table...knee-deep in scorpions....'

'Quick...quick...do something....Look out, look out!'

'Stop screeching and get a book, for God's

sake....You're worse than the dog.... Shut *up*, Roger....'

'By the Grace of God I wasn't bitten....'

'Look out...there's another one....Quick...quick....'

'Oh, shut up and get me a book or something....'

'But *how* did the scorpions get on the table, dear?'

'That bloody boy....Every matchbox in the house is a deathtrap....'

'Look out, it's coming towards me....Quick, quick, do something....'

'Hit it with your knife...*your knife*...Go on, hit it...'

Since no one had bothered to explain things to him, Roger was under the mistaken impression that the family were being attacked, and that it was his duty to defend them. As Lugaretzia was the only stranger in the room, he came to the logical conclusion that she must be the responsible party, so he bit her in the ankle. This did not help matters very much.

By the time a certain amount of order had been restored, all the baby scorpions had hidden themselves under various plates and bits of cutlery. Eventually, after impassioned pleas on my part, backed up by Mother, Leslie's suggestion that the whole lot be slaughtered was quashed. While the family, still simmering with rage and fright, retired to the drawing-room, I spent half an hour rounding up the babies, picking them up in a teaspoon, and returning them to their mother's back. Then I carried them outside on a saucer and, with the utmost reluctance, released them on the garden wall. Roger and I went and spent the afternoon on the hillside, for I felt it would be prudent to allow the family to have a siesta before seeing them again.

GERALD DURRELL

AFTER READING

1 In pairs, discuss what each family member's reaction to the scorpions tells us about each of their characters.

2 List five facts that you have learnt about scorpions as a result of reading this passage.

Discussion

1   This passage is remarkable for the detailed picture that it paints of the wall and of the plants and animals that live on it and in it. In pairs, discuss why the author uses the following descriptive phrases and the effect they have on the reader. Then, write down your answers:

- The whole surface was an intricate map of cracks
- the roofs of a hundred tiny toadstools
- a labyrinth of blackberry
- the beetles, rotund and neatly clad as business men
- a little black scorpion...neatly jointed as armour

Assignments

1   Working in groups of four, improvise the conversation that the members of the family, Margo, Leslie, Larry and Mother, might have had while Gerry spent the afternoon on the hillside. Perform your scene in front of the class. Then, working alone, write up your own version of the conversation.

2   Look again at the description of the wall and the scorpions. Gerald Durrell describes the creatures' habitat (the wall), their appearance, their movements and their characters. Using the same amount of detail, write a description of an animal that you know well.

SHOULD WE EAT MEAT?

■ This issue is explored in the poem 'Bags of Meat', and ignored in the McDonald's promotional leaflet 'Did you know?'

Bags of Meat

'Here's a fine bag of meat,'
Says the master-auctioneer,
As the timid, quivering steer,
Starting a couple of feet
At the prod of a drover's stick,
And trotting lightly and quick,
A ticket stuck on his rump,
Enters with a bewildered jump.

'Where he's lived lately, friends,
I'd live till lifetime ends:
They've a whole life everyday
Down there in the Vale, have they!
He'd be worth the money to kill
And give away Christmas for goodwill.'

'Now here's a heifer – worth more
Than bid, were she bone-poor;
Yet she's round as a barrel of beer';
'She's a plum,' said the second auctioneer.

'Now this young bull – for thirty pound?
Worth that to manure your ground!'
'Or to stand,' chimed the second one,
'And have his picter done!'

The beast was rapped on the horns and snout
To make him turn about.
'Well,' cried a buyer, 'another crown –
Since I've dragged here from Taunton Town!'

'That calf, she sucked three cows,
Which is not matched for bouse
In the nurseries of high life
By the first-born of a nobleman's wife!'
The stick falls, meaning, 'A true tale's told,'
On the buttock of the creature sold,
And the buyer leans over and snips
His mark on one of the animal's hips.

Each beast, when driven in,
Looks round at the ring of bidders there
With a much-amazed reproachful stare,
As at unnatural kin,
For bringing him to a sinister scene
So strange, unhomelike, hungry, mean;
His fate the while suspended between
A butcher, to kill out of hand,
And a farmer, to keep on the land;
One can fancy a tear runs down his face
When the butcher wins, and he's driven from the place.

THOMAS HARDY

AFTER READING

1 In groups of four, prepare a group reading of the poem, paying particular attention to volume, pace, clarity, and fluency. There are four speaking parts: the narrator, the auctioneer, the second auctioneer and the buyer. Perform your reading in front of another group, and discuss the different interpretations of the poem by the various groups.

2 In small groups discuss what point(s) you think the author is making in this poem.

■ McDonald's decribe the quality of the beef used in their beefburgers.

DID YOU KNOW?

100% PURE BEEF – The Facts

Food hygiene and quality have always been important to McDonald's.

There has been much debate recently regarding the quality of meat used in pre-cooked meals, convenience foods and in the fast service restaurant industry.

McDonald's attention to high standards in this area is not a debatable point.

ONLY prime cuts of lean forequarter and flank are used for their 100% pure beef hamburgers.

NO ADDITIVES NO FILLERS NO BINDERS NO FLAVOUR ENHANCERS

JUST 100% PURE BEEF

All McDonald's beef comes from EC-approved European suppliers. Every consignment of beef arriving at the meat plant is subject to a total of 36 separate quality control checks, carried out by a team of qualified technologists. If a consignment should fail on any one check – it will be rejected by McDonald's.

In addition, a Ministry of Agriculture representative visits the plant weekly, to monitor its hygiene standards, as well as the quality of the beef.

McDonald's commitment to quality is paramount throughout the production and preparation of all its products, to ensure that customers receive only the highest food and beverage.

AFTER READING

1 Are you convinced after reading this fact sheet that the beef is 100% pure?

COMPARE

Discussion

1   In pairs, write down the ways in which the auctioneers in the poem try to convince the buyers that the cows are good quality stock. Then list the points that are made in the McDonald's fact sheet to convince the reader that their beef is of 'paramount quality'. What similarities can you find?

2   In pairs, compare the language used in the poem and in the leaflet. What differences are there in

- the style (e.g. the complexity of words) of the poem and the leaflet
- the tone (the overall effect) of the poem and the leaflet.

On your own, write a comparison of the language used in the poem and in the leaflet.

Assignments

1   Who puts forward the better case – the auctioneers selling the cows or the writers of the fact sheet selling beef burgers? Write an essay on this subject.

2   What is your view? Should animals be slaughtered for meat? Research this issue, and make notes of the main arguments for and against eating meat. Write down your views and prepare for a debate on this issue.

3   Use the style of the McDonald's fact sheet to write an advertisement for a completely different product, e.g. a soft drink. Your advert must contain five of the following words or phrases: quality, high, pure, approved, paramount, quality control checks, qualified technologists.

VIEWS ON VIVISECTION

■ Arguments are put forward for and against the use of animals in medical research.

ANIMAL CRACKERS

My childhood was deprived of pets. My mother grew up on a lowland farm and felt it would be cruel to keep a dog in town. I once won a goldfish at a fair but it escaped while we were in the taxi home and strangely we never did find it. After that my sister had a tortoise but it went into hibernation and never came out. After that I rather gave up on animals.

At medical school I discovered that they do, however, have their uses. The armadillo, for some reason, is ideally suited to leprosy research. Guinea pigs have an enzyme in their gut which makes them particularly suitable for studies on digestion. Dogs are prone to diabetes. Pigs are immunologically very similar to humans and are used in transplant studies. You can test anaesthetics on sheep. Cats get a virus that is very similar to Aids. You can give colds and measles to ferrets. At Harvard they've patented a strain of mice which are guaranteed to get cancer by the age of 90 days.

You may, understandably, want to distance yourself from this kind of thing, but then again you may not realise how much our comfortable lives really owe to animal experimentation. Animal research is used in the development of pesticides and fertilisers. Every garment you wear that has been treated with chemicals or dyed with synthetic dyes was tested on animals. Every drug, every food additive, almost every cosmetic you use has, somewhere down the line, been safety-tested on animals. Most medical treatments and surgical procedures were tested first on animals. The only way you could be free of products tested on animals is to live naked on an island off Papua New Guinea... and not use any sun-tan lotion.

From the sheer scale of our debt to animals, one might assume that they are being massacred at a wholesale rate in labs all over Britain. In fact, the number of animals annually martyred to science stands at 3.2 million. This compares with the 500 million animals annually slaughtered for food in Britain or the 1,000 dogs a day put down. By comparison, our national consumption of laboratory animals, in per capita terms, is one mouse per person every 15 years.

I use the mouse advisedly here. Eighty per cent of animals used in research are mice or rats. Anything larger tends to make too much mess, eat too much food and blunder into the computers. They are also rather difficult to hide.

The reason you'd want to hide a laboratory animal is not because you're doing anything underhand to it. Lab animals are housed by law in five-star accommodation, are looked after by experienced handlers and have a vet in regular atttendance. They are protected by the Animals (Scientific Procedures) Act 1986, a piece of legislation unique to Britain which ensures that laboratory animals get a much better deal than my goldfish or tortoise ever did. The reason they need to be hidden is to protect them from the mad people in balaclavas.

These are the people who, not long ago, torched the Parke Davis laboratory in Cambridge, barbecuing most of the resident animals. These are the people who 'liberated' a number of sleepy experimental rats from the Huntington Research Centre so they could be mown down on the neighbouring A1. The campaign of terror they wage against committed and humane scientific people is not even funny. These people are nutcases.

What's unfortunate is that their activities have overshadowed the valuable work done in this country by animal welfare organisations, the majority of whom recognise that a number of experiments are

unavoidable. At some point a new drug or chemical has to be administered to humans and it would be foolhardy not to try it out on animals first. What they have campaigned for, and what the law now aims to ensure, is that experiments are performed only by experts, that they don't cause prolonged suffering and that they are never performed unnecessarily.

There used to be quite a lot of unnecessary research on animals. Many 'new' products are not new at all and testing them on animals merely re-established the old findings. In recognition of this, and in response to public pressure, animal testing on new cosmetics has fallen in the last couple of years by about two-thirds. Animal testing has been further reduced by the discovery of test-tube alternatives. The standard test for the purity of manufactured insulin used to be the 'mouse convulsion test', in which insulin was administered to mice until they had a fit. This has been superseded by simple blood sampling of the test mice and, recently, by direct chemical analysis of the insulin.

As science becomes more sophisticated the use of animals has become more refined. Laboratory animals are now investigated rather like patients in hospitals, with the use of anaesthetics and painkillers. Their pulse and blood pressure and respiration are measured by non-invasive instruments. Anything which will cause them distress is usually avoided. This is as much

1 What reasons does Dr Collee give for calling the animal liberationists 'mad people in balaclavas' and 'nutcases'?

2 Have your views about the use of animals in medical research changed as a result of reading this article?

■ The argument against animal experimentation.

for practical as legal reasons. If you've ever tried to shampoo a dog you will know how a struggling animal can screw up the whole experiment.

Contrary to popular belief, gratuitous cruelty to laboratory animals in Britain is virtually unknown, whereas cruelty to household pets is an everyday occurrence. There's a dog that's dragged round my local park every day, constantly yelled at and psychologically abused by its tyrannical owner. If I was that dog, I don't think I'd be any worse off in some comfortable lab where I could test moisturising cream and have my blood pressure reduced.　●

JOHN COLLEE
THE OBSERVER MAGAZINE

BRITISH UNION FOR THE ABOLITION OF VIVISECTION

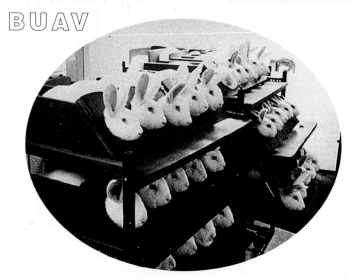

Campaigning to end animal experiments

In 1989 over 12,000 animals including rabbits, guinea pigs, mice and rats were used to test cosmetics, toiletries and their ingredients in British laboratories. Rabbits had substances dripped into their unprotected eyes and the effects – including swelling, redness and ulceration – were studied. In other tests animals had their fur shaved, skin broken and products rubbed into their raw backs, causing inflammation, cracking and bleeding. Animals were also force-fed or injected with substances causing poisoning and death.

Thousands of wild monkeys are cruelly trapped, packed into tiny wooden crates and flown thousands of miles to be used in crude, cruel experiments in British laboratories every year. Most of the monkeys that are captured never make it that far. As many as nine out of ten die of disease, are killed during trapping or are slaughtered by dealers because they are unsuitable for laboratory needs – being too young, too old or pregnant.

The survivors suffer the loss of their jungle homes in countries such as Indonesia and the Philippines, in exchange for a cramped bare metal cage, despair and death.

Once wild and free, these sensitive and intelligent animals end their short lives as living test-tubes – force-fed chemicals, dosed with drugs or used in other painful and pointless tests.

It's a far cry from the Paradise they have lost.

PLEASE HELP US BREAK THIS CHAIN OF MISERY. SEND OFF FOR YOUR FREE INFORMATION PACK TODAY.

AFTER READING

1 Would the arguments put forward in this advert make you want to support this pressure group? Why or why not?

2 How would the BUAV like readers to react to their advertisement? Choose three words to describe the way the advertisement is supposed to make us feel.

COMPARE

Discussion

1   Look again at the two passages. Make a list of the words that the writers use to get the reader to agree with them. Set out your lists like this, one list for each passage.

BUAV	Animal Crackers
trapped	five-star accommodation

Which passage uses the most emotive words?

2   What else do the writers use to persuade us of their opinions – tone, style, etc? Discuss your ideas with the rest of the class.

Assignments

1   List what you think are the three main arguments from each passage for and against the use of animals in experiments. For each point, write down your own opinion as well.

2   Several horror films are based on a plot of animals taking revenge upon humans for the way that they are treated by them. This can happen in reality!

MUTANT TURTLE TERROR THREATENS RIVIERA BATHERS
Thousands of miniature turtles bought as children's pets at the height of the Mutant Ninja Turtle craze are turning into monsters in the south of France, biologists warned yesterday.
Abandoned by being flushed down the lavatory or discarded in lakes, the little terrapins only a few inches long are mutating into carnivorous creatures weighing up to 10 *lb* and over a foot long. (The *Guardian*)

Continue this report using your own words and ideas.

1 How successfully did the authors of the books that you have read convey the feelings and the thoughts of animals?

2 Write your own story in which animals have the characteristics of human beings.

WIDER READING

Stories about animals
Richard Adams, *Watership Down* and *The Plague Dogs*; Paul Gallico, *The Snow Goose*; Jack London, *White Fang*; James Herriot, *It Shouldn't Happen to a Vet*; Daphne du Maurier, *The Birds*.

Stories with animal characters
Kenneth Graham, *Wind in The Willows*; Robert C O'Brien, *Mrs Frisby and the Rats of Nimh*; Richard Adams, *Watership Down*; George Orwell, *Animal Farm*; R.K. Narayan, *Tiger for Malgudi*.

LEGEND

- *Which of these definitions is closest to your understanding of the word legend?*
- *What 'ingredients' should a legend have?*

HANDLE WITH CARE

■ These two very famous stories end with quite different moods – one of possible misery and the other of power and hope.

READING SKILLS

Analysing language

Pandora's Box

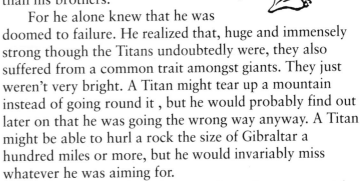

THERE are some who say that the original creator of mankind was Prometheus, that he fashioned the first man in the image of the gods using clay and water taken from Panopeus in Phocis. Prometheus was a Titan, one of the race of giants who fought an unsuccessful war against Zeus and the other gods – and it is certainly true that he was a great deal wiser than his brothers.

For he alone knew that he was doomed to failure. He realized that, huge and immensely strong though the Titans undoubtedly were, they also suffered from a common trait amongst giants. They just weren't very bright. A Titan might tear up a mountain instead of going round it , but he would probably find out later on that he was going the wrong way anyway. A Titan might be able to hurl a rock the size of Gibraltar a hundred miles or more, but he would invariably miss whatever he was aiming for.

On the other hand, of course, the gods were as quick-witted as they were skilled in the art of war. First there was Zeus, the king of Olympus, armed with his devastating thunderbolts. Then there was Poseidon with his trident, Apollo with his golden arrows, the invisible Hermes...it was an invincible army and Prometheus could see that his brothers would be lost against it.

Lose was what they did. Most of them were sent to a dark and damp prison in the depths of Tartarus. Atlas – perhaps the most famous Titan of all – was condemned to hold up the heavens on his shoulders for all time. But Prometheus, who had let everyone know that he was neutral from the start, got away scot-free. That was when he created man.

Prometheus loved men in the same way people love their pets. He was immensely proud of everything they did, boasted about them to almost anyone who would listen, and generally fussed over them in every way possible. Instead of feeding them with food, however, he fed them knowledge – scraps of information that he picked up from Athene, the goddess of wisdom and his only real friend in Olympus. One day she would tell him about mathematics and straight away he would rush down to earth to pass it on. The next day it might be art or architecture, the day after that science or engineering. It's strange to think that our entire civilization could have been handed down to us rather in the manner of dog biscuits, but that is how it was.

As the years passed and mankind became more intelligent, Zeus, who had been watching all this from his celestial throne, grew uneasy.

"I am a little worried about these human beings," he remarked to his wife, Hera, one day over a goblet of wine.

"What about them?" Hera asked.

"Well...I just wonder if they're not getting a bit...above themselves. Where will it lead to? That's what I want to know. Today the rudiments of geometry, tomorrow it could be genetic surgery."

"So what are you going to do about it?"

"I don't know. But I'm keeping my eye on them!"

Zeus might have been a jealous god, but he was not cruel enough to destroy the newly formed human race. And so mankind continued to flourish. Things came to a head, however, one day in a place called Sicyon. The trouble was caused by a question of ownership.

Prometheus had taught man to stay on the right side of the gods by regularly sacrificing the best animals from their herds. A special sacrificial bull had been chosen for

Zeus at Sicyon, but the question was, which part should be reserved for the god and which parts should the men (who had worked hard to raise the animal in the first place) be allowed to keep? As usual Prometheus acted as the mediator in the dispute but, unwisely, he decided to play a trick on Zeus.

When the bull had been killed and cut up, he took two sacks. Into one of these, he put all the most succulent portions of meat – the rump and the fillet, the sirloin and the rib – but concealed them beneath the stomach-bag which was all white and rubbery and generally disgusting to look at. Into the other went the bones and the gristle, the eyeballs and the hooves...in short all the most unappetizing parts of the bull. But these were covered with a layer of fat to make them look as delicious as possible.

Then Prometheus took both sacks and knelt before Zeus.

"Oh mighty king!" he said. "Why should there be any quarrel between you and the little pink creatures who inhabit the world below? Take this matter of sacrifice. It seems that nobody can decide who should get exactly what. Well, as you are the king of Olympus, why don't you choose for yourself? I have divided the bull between these two sacks. Which one do you want?"

Zeus, who had never suspected that a Titan could think up such a scheme, was completely deceived. He chose the bones and the fat. Ever since that time the gods have received nothing else from the sacrifice. When he found out how Prometheus had tricked him, however, he was furious.

"Man may have his steak," he thundered. "But he will eat it raw!"

And with those words, he reached out with one hand and snatched all the fire from the world.

It seemed that mankind had got the worst deal after all. Without fire they could take no pleasure in their food, and once the sun had gone down, they could only stay indoors, huddled under animal skins for warmth. But Prometheus was willing to do anything to help his creation and one day, while Zeus was out having one of his many affairs, he stole up to Olympus. For he still had one friend in the home of the gods: Athene. Hearing him knocking on a side-door, the goddess of wisdom unbolted it and let him in. Then Prometheus rode up to the sun and, using his bare hands, broke off a blazing fire-brand. This he carried back to earth, thrusting it into a giant fennel-leaf. And in this way people were once again able to enjoy their meat *grillé*.

But this time Prometheus had gone too far. When Zeus heard how he had been defied for a second time, his anger knew no bounds.

"Prometheus!" he cried. "You crossed me once and I forgave you because of your loyalty to me in the war of the Titans. But this time there can be no forgiveness. This time you must pay for your crime."

And so saying, he seized Prometheus and chained him to a pillar on the freezing slopes of the Caucasian mountains. But if this was not punishment enough, worse was to come. Every morning a huge vulture landed on the wretched Titan's chest and even as he screamed in rage and horror, tore out his liver and devoured it. And every night, while Prometheus shivered in the sub-zero temperatures, his liver grew whole again. In this way the horrible torture could be repeated again and again until the end of time.

Zeus punished mankind too. But as man had only offended indirectly, his punishment was of another sort.

First he visited the crippled god Hephaestus who worked at a great forge in Olympus with twenty bellows pumping twenty-four hours a day. Although ugly and misshapen himself, no blacksmith was more skilled than Hephaestus.

"I want you to make me a woman," the king of the gods commanded. "I want her to be more beautiful than any woman ever seen on the face of the earth. She must be perfect. As perfect as a goddess."

Hephaestus did as he was told. He had only ever disobeyed Zeus once. That had been just before he became the crippled god. Now he fashioned a woman out of clay, moulding her perfect features with his own hands. He commissioned the four winds to breathe life into her and asked all the goddesses to help dress her in their finest clothes and jewels.

The result was Pandora.

When Zeus saw the blacksmith-god's work he was well pleased and instructed Hermes to carry her into the world at once. There she was married to a certain King Epimetheus, the brother of Prometheus and the only other Titan who had not joined in the war against the gods.

Now Epimetheus had been warned never to trust the gifts of Zeus, but seeing the terrible fate that had befallen his brother, he was too afraid to refuse. Moreover, he had to admit that Pandora was beautiful. You'd have had to be mad to think otherwise. When she walked into the room, men fell silent and all eyes turned on her. Whatever she said, people would agree. When she made jokes, the laughter would continue for several minutes. Whatever she did was greeted with applause. And Epimetheus did feel rather proud to be married to her.

Unfortunately, the things Pandora said were never really worth listening to, for she was not a very intelligent creature. Her jokes were in truth extremely unfunny. She did very little because she was impossibly lazy and if Epimetheus was glad to be her husband, she made him a poor and unfaithful wife. For this was the revenge of Zeus. He had made her as shallow and as coquettish as she was beautiful. And she was to cause more trouble to mankind than any woman before or any woman since.

For Epimetheus owned a large, ebony box which was kept in a special room in his palace, guarded day and night. In this box he had collected and imprisoned all the things that could harm mankind. It was the one room in the palace that Pandora was forbidden to enter and naturally it was the one room that most aroused her curiosity.

"I bet you keep all sorts of super things in that big, black box of yours," she would say in her syrupy voice. "Why don't you let your little Pandy look inside?"

"It is not for you, my dear," Epimetheus would reply. "You should leave well alone."

"But..."

"No, no, my love. No one may open the box."

"Then you don't love me," Pandora would say, crossing her arms and pouting. "And I'm not going to love you any more – not ever!"

They had this conversation many times until the day when Pandora couldn't resist her curiosity any longer. For despite everything Epimetheus had told her about the box, she still believed that it contained some special treat that he was holding back from her.

"I'll show him...the old bossy-boots," she muttered to herself.

Waiting until Epimetheus was out, she managed to talk her way past the guards and into the room. She had stolen the key from beside his bed and nobody thought to stop her. Was she not, after all, the king's wife and the mistress of the house? Her whole body trembling, she knelt down beside the box. It was smaller and older than she had expected. It was also a little surprising (not to say upsetting) that the padlock which fastened it should be in the shape of a human skull. But she was certain it would contain treasure such as would make all her own diamonds and pearls seem like mere pebbles, treasure that would make her the envy of the world. She turned the key and opened the box...

...and at once all the spites and problems that Epimetheus had for so long kept locked up, exploded into the world. Old age, hard work, sickness... they flew out in a great cloud of buzzing, stinging, biting insects. It was as if Pandora had accidentally split the atom. One moment she was standing there with a foolish grin on her face. The next she was screaming in the heart of an intense darkness that had, in seconds, stripped her of her beauty and brought her out in a thousand boils.

At that moment, all the things that make life difficult today streamed out of Pandora's box and into the world.

Old age, hard work, sickness, vice, anger, envy, lust, covetousness, spite, sarcasm, cynicism, violence, intolerance, injustice, infidelity, famine, drought, pestilence, war, religious persecution, apartheid, taxation, inflation, pollution, unemployment, fascism, racism, sexism, terrorism, communism, nepotism, cubism, patriotism, nihilism, totalitarianism, plagiarism, vandalism, tourism, paranoia, schizophrenia, kleptomania, claustrophobia, xenophobia, hypochondria, insomnia, megalomania, narrow-mindedness, thoughtlessness, selfishness, bribery, corruption, censorship, gluttony, pornography, delinquency, vulgarity, bureaucracy, complacency, obesity, acne, diplomatic immunity, traffic congestion, party political broadcasts, urban development, modern architecture, fast food, muzak, dolphinariums, organized crime, advertising, alcoholism, drug addiction, monosodium glutamate, nicotine, nuclear waste, data processing, fanaticism, insanity, drizzle, elephant's-feet-wastepaper-baskets and much, much more.

At the last moment, Epimetheus managed to slam down the lid, by which time only one thing was left in the box: hope.

Which is just as well. For with all the problems that Pandora had released into the world, where would we be without it?

ANTHONY HOROWITZ

AFTER READING

1 Think of three words to describe the character of Zeus.

2 Now think of three words to describe Pandora.

The Sword in the Stone ❧

Then Merlin went to the archbishop of Canterbury, and counselled him for to send for all the lords of the realm, and all the gentlemen of arms, that they should to London come by Christmas upon pain of cursing: and for this cause – that Jesus, that was born on that night, that he would of his great mercy shew some miracle, as he was come to be king of mankind, for to shew some miracle who should be rightwise king of this realm. So the archbishop by the advice of Merlin sent for all the lords and gentlemen of arms, that they should come by Christmas even unto London.... And when matins and the first mass was done, there was seen in the churchyard against the high altar a great stone four square, like unto a marble stone, and in the midst thereof was like an anvil of steel a foot on high, and therein stack a fair sword naked by the point, and letters there were written in gold about the sword that said thus: Whoso pulleth out this sword of this stone and anvil is rightwise king born of all England....

So when all masses were done all the lords went to behold the stone and the sword. And when they saw the scripture, some assayed – such as would have been king. But none might stir the sword nor move it. He is not here, said the archbishop, that shall achieve the sword, but doubt not God will make him known....

So upon New Year's Day when the service was done the barons rode to the field, some to just, and some to tourney; and so it happened that Sir Ector, that had great livelihood about London, rode unto the justs, and with him rode Sir Kay his son and young Arthur that was his nourished brother, and Sir Kay was made knight at All-hallowmas afore. So as they rode to the justs-ward Sir Kay had lost his sword, for he had left it at his father's lodging, and so he prayed young Arthur to ride for his sword. I will well, said Arthur, and rode fast after the sword; and when he came home the lady and all were out to see the justing. Then was Arthur wroth, and said to himself, I will ride to the churchyard and take the sword with me that sticketh in the stone, for my brother Sir Kay shall not be without a sword this day. So when he came to the churchyard Sir Arthur alighted, and tied the horse to the stile, and so he went to the tent, and found no knights there, for they were at the justing; and so he handled the sword by the handles, and lightly and fiercely pulled it out of the stone, and took his horse and rode his way till he came to his brother Sir Kay, and delivered him the sword. And as soon as Sir Kay saw the sword he wist well it was the sword of the stone, and so he rode to his father Sir Ector, and said: Sir, lo here is the sword of the stone; wherefore I must be king of this land. When Sir Ector beheld the sword he returned again and came to the church, and there they alighted all three and went into the church, and anon he made Sir Kay to swear upon a book how he came to that sword. Sir, said Sir Kay, by my brother Arthur, for he brought it to me. How gat ye this sword? said Sir Ector to Arthur. Sir, I will tell you: when I came home for my brother's sword, I found nobody at home to deliver me his sword, and so I thought my brother Sir Kay should not be swordless, and so I came hither eagerly and pulled it out of the stone without any pain. Found ye any knights about this sword? said Sir Ector. Nay, said Arthur. Now, said Sir Ector to Arthur, I understand you must be king of this land. Wherefore I, said Arthur, and for what cause? Sir, said

Ector, for God will have it so: for there should never man have drawn out this sword but he that shall be rightwise king of this land. Now let me see whether ye can put the sword there as it was, and pull it out again. That is no mastery, said Arthur: and so he put it into the stone. Therewith Sir Ector assayed to pull out the sword and failed.

HOW KING ARTHUR PULLED OUT THE SWORD DIVERS TIMES.

Now assay, said Sir Ector to Sir Kay. And anon he pulled at the sword with all his might, but it would not be. Now shall ye assay, said Sir Ector to Arthur. I will well, said Arthur, and pulled it out easily. And therewithal Sir Ector kneeled down to the earth, and Sir Kay. Alas, said Arthur, mine own dear father and brother, why kneel ye to me. Nay, nay, my lord Arthur, it is not so: I was never your father nor of your blood, but I wote well ye are of an higher blood than I wend ye were. And then Sir Ector told him all, how he was betaken him for to nourish him, and by whose commandment, and by Merlin's deliverance. Then Arthur made great dole when he understood that Sir Ector was not his father. Sir, said Ector unto Arthur, will ye be my good and gracious lord when ye are king? Else were I to blame, said Arthur, for ye are the man in the world that I am most beholding to, and my good lady and mother your wife, that as well as her own hath fostered me and kept. And if ever it be God's will that I be king, as ye say, ye shall desire of me what I may do, and I shall not fail you: God forbid I should fail you.

THOMAS MALLORY
LA MORTE D'ARTHUR

1 In three or four sentences try to summarise what happens.

2 Find five words to show that the legend was told long ago.

COMPARE

Discussion

1 Look at the beginnings of both passages. Which one makes you want to read on more? Discuss why this is, paying attention to content, words and sentence structure.

2 Discuss which story:
- is more serious
- is more descriptive
- is more realistic
- has the stronger characterisation

Then in small groups present your ideas to the rest of the class, giving examples to support your conclusions.

3 Discuss the use of humour in the telling of *Pandora's Box*. At which points does the writer use humour? What effect does it have in the way we respond to the characters? Does it make the story less believable overall? Would the use of humour have improved the King Arthur extract?

Assignments

1 Take the first few paragraphs of the King Arthur legend and rewrite it. How would you tell the story in more modern English, perhaps to children aged 7 to 11? Which words would you have to change? How would you change the structure? Have a go, and see what the effect is.

2 Write a follow-up story, either about what happens next to King Arthur, or the effect that opening Pandora's box has on the world.

3 Report the events of one of the stories as if it was a special news broadcast. For example, imagine a reporter witnessing King Arthur pulling the sword from the stone; or an eyewitness account of Pandora opening the box. Write a script which recounts the events from the point of view of journalists and eyewitnesses, making it as factual and as serious in tone as possible.

LEGENDS WORLDWIDE

■ This first folk tale comes from Japan.

READING SKILLS

Developing personal response

Reading for meaning

Reading aloud

The Mirror

There is a pretty Japanese tale of a small farmer who bought his young wife a mirror. She was surprised and delighted to know that it reflected her face, and cherished her mirror above all her possessions. She gave birth to one daughter, and died young; and the farmer put the mirror away in a press, where it lay for long years.

The daughter grew up the very image of her mother; and one day, when she was almost a woman, her father took her aside, and told her of her mother,

and of the mirror which had reflected her beauty. The girl was devoured with curiosity, unearthed the mirror from the old press, and looked into it.

'Father!' she cried, 'See! Here is mother's face!'

It was her own face she saw; but her father said nothing.

The tears were streaming down his cheeks, and the words would not come.

Midwife and the Frog

My grandmother's mother was a midwife – the queen's midwife, as we used to say, because she drew her pay from the parish, which in our eyes meant the whole country.

One night she was called away to assist at a childbirth. It was about midnight. It was pitch dark on the road and it was raining. When the woman was delivered of her babe – God let her have a good one – my great-grandmother started off homeward. On the road she came across a big frog. It was hopping along right in front of her. My great-grandmother had always had a holy fear of frogs, and she cried out in terror, 'Get out of my way, you hideous creature! Why on earth are you hopping around me? Is it a midwife you may be wanting?'

And thus she was conversing with the frog as she proceeded on her way, and the frog jumped closer and closer to her. Once it got right under her feet, and she stepped on it. It gave such a shriek that my great-grandmother almost jumped out of her shoes. Well, she went home leaving the frog on the road, and the frog hopped off to some place, wherever it had its abode.

Back at home, my great-grandmother went to bed.

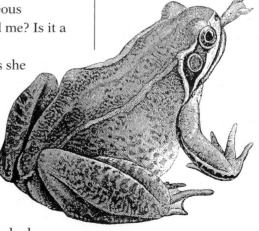

Suddenly she heard a cart driving into the yard. She thought there was another childbirth where her assistance would be needed. Soon she saw the door open. Two men came in, both very dark-skinned. They were both spindleshanks; their legs looked like a pair of pipestems, and their heads were as big as a bushel. They greeted her with, 'Good evening,' and then said, 'We want to take you along, mother; you must come and help with a birth.'

She said, 'Who is it?' as it is the custom of a midwife to enquire where her assistance is wanted.

One of the men said, 'On the road you promised my wife to help her with the child when her time came.'

And this gave my great-grandmother something to think of, because she had not met a single soul on her way back, except the frog. 'It's true,' she thought to herself, 'I asked her by way of a joke "Is it a midwife you're looking for? I might come and help you too."'

The two men said to her, 'Do not tarry, mother.'

But she said to them, 'I'm not going with you because I've met no human creature and I've promised nothing.'

But they were so insistent that she should keep her promise that finally she said, 'Well, as you are so keen on taking me along, I'll go with you.'

She thought to herself that in any case she'd take her rosary with her, and that if she would pray, God would not forsake her, wherever she'd be taken by the two men. And then the men left her alone, and she began to dress. She dressed herself quite neatly, and when she was ready she asked the men, 'Is it a long journey? Shall I put on more warm clothes?'

'We aren't going far. It will take us an hour and a half or so to get back. But hurry up, mother, because my wife was in a bad state when I left her.'

Then she finished dressing and went out with the two men. They put her in their black coach and soon were driving up a big mountain. It was Magyarós Mountain, not far from the backs of the Szucsáva. As they were driving along, suddenly the mountain opened up before them, and they drove straight through the split, right into the centre of the mountain. They pulled up before a house and one of the men opened the door for her.

'Well, you go in to her,' he said. 'You'll find my wife there. She's lying on the floor.'

And as she stepped through the door, she beheld a small

woman lying on the floor. She, too, had a head as big as a bushel. She looked ill and was groaning terribly.

My great-grandmother said to her, 'You're in a bad state, daughter, aren't you? But have no fear, God will deliver you of your burden, and then you'll feel well again.'

The woman said to my great-grandmother, 'Don't say that God will help me. My husband must not hear you saying it.'

The midwife asked, 'What else could I say?'

'Say the *gyivák* [a type of devil] will help you.'

Then my great-grandmother – we had it from her own mouth – felt as if the words had frozen on her lips, so alarmed did she grow at the thought of what place she had been brought to. No sooner had she thought about it than the child was born, a spindleshanks, with legs as thin as pipestems and a head as big as a stewpot. My great-grandmother thought to herself, 'Well, I was brought here, but how am I to get back?' So she turned to the woman. 'Well, your men have brought me to your place, but how can I get back? It's pitch dark outside. I couldn't find my way back home alone.'

The sick woman then said, 'Do not worry about that. My husband will take you back to the same place he brought you from.' And then she asked my great-grandmother, 'Well, mother, do you know who I am?'

'I couldn't say I do. I've asked your husband a few questions about you, but he didn't tell me a thing. He said I should go with them and I'd learn in time who you were.'

'Well, you know who I am? I am the frog you kicked about on the road and trod under your feet. Now, this should serve as a lesson that if you happen to come across some creature like me at about midnight or an hour past it, do not speak to it, nor take heed of what you see. Just pass along on your way. You see, you stopped to talk to me and made a promise to me. So you had to be brought here, because I was that frog you met on the road.'

Then my great-grandmother said, 'I've done my job here; now get me back to my home.'

Then the man came in and asked her, 'Well, what would you want me to pay for your troubles?'

Then the old midwife said, 'I don't want you to pay me anything. Get me right back to the place you brought me from.'

The man said, 'Do not worry. We still have half an hour

or so to get you back. But now let me take you to our larder so that you may see for yourself that we are doing well. You needn't fear that we haven't the wherewithal to pay for your services.'

And my great-grandmother followed him to the larder. In the larder she beheld all sorts of food heaped on the shelves: flour and bacon and firkins of lard here, and loaves of bread and cream there and a lot of other things, all arranged in neat order, to say nothing of veritable mounds of gold and silver.

'Now you can see for yourself what plenty there is. Whatever the rich men and the wealthy farmers deny to the poor in their greed becomes ours and goes into our storeroom.' And he turned to my great-grandmother and said, 'Well, mother, let's get along. There isn't much time left for us to get you back to your home. Take of this gold an apronful, as I see you have on your Sunday apron.'

And he insisted on her taking an apronful of gold. He wouldn't let her leave the larder until she had filled her apron with it.

When she had put the fold in her apron, she was taken to the top of Magyarós Mountain by the same coach in which she had first come. But dawn was already coming on, and soon the cock uttered its first crow. Then the men pushed her from the black coach – though they were still near the top – and said to her, 'Trot along, mother, you can find your way home from here.'

And when she took a look at her apron to make sure that she had the gold, there was nothing whatever in her apron; that heap of gold had vanished into thin air.

And that is all there is to the story; you can take it from me.

AFTER READING

1 What is the basic storyline here? Identify the main events in the tale.

2 How would you describe the characters of the great-grandmother and the pregnant woman?

GELERT, LLEWELYN'S DOG

■ This eighteenth-century ballad from Wales tells the famous tale of one person's disastrous misunderstanding of events. For best effect, work in groups to prepare a choral reading of different verses of the poem.

The spearmen heard the bugle sound,
And cheerily smiled the morn.
And many a brach and many a hound
Attend Llewelyn's horn.

And still he blew a louder blast,
And gave a louder cheer –
Come Gelert! Why art thou the last
Llewelyn's horn to hear?

Oh where does faithful Gelert roam?
The flower of his race!
So true so brave! a lamb at home.
A lion in the chase.

'Twas only at Llewelyn's board
The faithful Gelert fed.
He watched, he served, he cheered his lord,
And sentinel'd his bed.

In sooth he was a peerless hound,
The gift of Royal John –
But now no Gelert could be found,
And all the chase rode on.

And now as over rocks and dells
The gallant chidings rise,
All Snowdon's craggy chaos yells
With many mingled cries.

That day Llewelyn little moved
The chase of hart or hare,
And scant and small the booty proved
For Gelert was not there.

Unpleased Llewelyn homeward hied.
When near the portal seat,
His truant, Gelert, he espied,
Bounding his lord to greet.

But when he gained his castle door,
Aghast the chieftan stood,
The hound all o'er was smeared with gore,
His lips, his fangs, ran blood.

Llewelyn gazed with wild surprise
Unused such looks to meet,
His favourite checked his joyful guise
And crouched and licked his foot.

Onward in haste Llewelyn passed –
And on went Gelert too –
And still where'er his eyes were cast
Fresh blood-gouts shocked his view.

O'erturned his infant's bed he found!
The blood-stained covert rent,
And all around the walls and ground,
With recent blood besprent!

He called his child – no voice replied!
He searched with terror wild.
Blood, blood, he found on every side!
But nowhere found his child!

Hell hound! my child's by thee devoured
The frantic father cried.
And to the hilt his vengeful sword
He plunged in Gelert's side.

His suppliant look, as to earth he fell,
No pity could impart,
But still his Gelert's dying yell
Past heavy o'er his heart.

Aroused by Gelert's dying yell
Some slumberer wakened nigh,
What words the parent's joy can tell
To hear his infant cry.

Concealed beneath a mangled heap
His hurried search had missed,
All glowing from his rosy sleep
His cherub boy he kissed!

Nor scratch had he, nor harm nor dread
But the same couch beneath
Lay a great wolf, all torn and dead –
Tremendous still in death.

Ah! what was then Llewelyn's pain
For now the truth was clear;
The gallant hound the wolf had slain
To save Llewelyn's heir.

Vain, vain was all of Llewelyn's woe
Best of all thy kind, adieu!
The frantic deed which had laid thee low
This heart shall ever rue!

And now a gallant tomb they rise
With costly sculpture decked,
And marbles storied with his praise
Poor Gelert's bones protect.

Here never could a spearman pass,
Or forester, unmoved.
Here oft the tear-besprinkled grass
Llewelyn's sorrow proved.

And here he hung his horn and spear
And oft as evening fell,
In fancy's piercing sounds would bear
Poor Gelert's dying yell.

W R SPENCER

AFTER READING

1 How effective was your group reading in terms of volume, clarity, pace and fluency?

2 Finish each of these statements about the poem:
- At the start of the poem Llewelyn is unhappy with the day's hunting because...
- Once home, Llewelyn's first thought is...
- He realizes his mistake when...
- What had in fact happened was...
- To show his shame and grief publicly, Llewelyn...

COMPARE

Discussion

1   Look at this list of some folk tale ingredients:

- we are not given much detail about the characters
- there is little description of place
- the story is told in a spoken rather than written style
- there is often a moral or a message
- people suffer for their mistakes

Apply each statement in turn to the three stories.

2   Which of these words best describe the great-grandmother and Llewelyn (a) at the start of the stories and (b) by the end. Choose as many as you like:

wealthy, foolish, quick-tempered, devoted, aggressive, humiliated, upset, distraught, sorry, self-confident, proud, grieving, regretful.

Are there any other, more accurate, words you would want to use?

3   Look again at the first paragraph of each passage. Try to summarise, as precisely as you can, how the styles of the storytellers differ.

4   What elements of mystery or of the unexpected do the three stories contain?

5   Discuss which story you enjoyed more, giving clear reasons.

Assignments

1   Based on the stories you have read and on the suggestions below, write your own folk tale:

- choose two main characters who will come into conflict (e.g. parent and foolish child; lazy wizard and ambitious helper; evil adult and innocent child)
- decide upon an event or conflict which will be the central point of the story
- avoid giving too much description; concentrate on telling the story.

2   Choose one of the three folk tales, and rewrite it as a play for radio, paying close attention to use of sound effects and voices to build atmosphere.

Use the characters' initial letters to indicate their lines in the script, and underline or italicize instructions and sound effects like this:

Ll: *Sound of bugle and hounds barking.* Come, Gelert!

You might find it useful to include a narrator or storyteller as one of your characters.

3   Research a legend from your local area, and tell the story in a narrative poem. Look at the Wider Reading list for some poems you might use as models.

4   Using encyclopaedias or language reference books, do some research into the history of the oral tradition – stories handed down through the centuries by word of mouth. Then write a brief account of the importance of storytelling before the invention of the printed word.

MODERN MYTHS

■ The following newspaper report about a rabbit falling to a concrete mixer caught the imagination of poet Roger McGough. He retells the story from the rabbit's point of view.

AFTER READING

1 What are the three main facts of the story?

2 Pick out three key words or phrases which show that this story appeared in a newspaper rather than in a work of fiction.

RABBIT IN MIXER SURVIVES

A baby rabbit fell into a quarry's mixing machine yesterday and came out in the middle of a concrete block. But the rabbit still had the strength to dig its way free before the block set.

The tiny creature was scooped up with 30 tons of sand, then swirled and pounded through the complete mixing process. Mr Michael Hooper, the machine operator, found the rabbit shivering on top of the solid concrete block, its coat stiff with fragments. A hole from the middle of the block and paw marks showed the escape route.

Mr Reginald Denslow, manager of J R Pratt and Sons' quarry at Kilmington, near Axminster, Devon, said: 'This rabbit must have a lot more than nine lives to go through this machine. I just don't know how it avoided being suffocated, ground, squashed or cut in half.' With the 30 tons of sand, it was dropped into a weighing hopper and carried by conveyor to an overhead mixer where it was whirled around with gallons of water.

From there the rabbit was swept to a machine which hammers wet concrete into blocks by pressure of 100 lb per square inch. The rabbit was encased in a block eighteen inches long, nine inches high and six inches thick. Finally the blocks were ejected on to the floor to dry and the dazed rabbit clawed itself free. 'We cleaned him up, dried him by the electric fire, then he hopped away,' Mr Denslow said.

ARTICLE PUBLISHED IN THE DAILY TELEGRAPH

Rabbit in mixer survives

'Tell us a story Grandad'
The bunny rabbits implored
'About the block of concrete
Out of which you clawed.'

'Tell every gory detail
Of how you struggled free
From the teeth of the Iron Monster

And swam through a quicksand sea.'
'How you battled with the Humans
(And the part we like the most)
Your escape from the raging fire
When they held you there to roast.'

The old adventurer smiled
And waved a wrinkled paw
'All right children, settle down
I'll tell it just once more.'

His thin nose started twitching
Near-blind eyes began to flood
As the part that doesn't age
Drifted back to bunnyhood.

When spring was king of the seasons
And days were built to last
When thunder was merely thunder
Not a distant quarry blast.

How, leaving the warren one morning
Looking for somewhere to play,
He'd wandered far into the woods
And there had lost his way.

When suddenly without warning
The earth gave way, and he fell
Off the very edge of the world
Into the darkness of Hell.

Sharp as the colour of a carrot
On a new-born bunny's tongue
Was the picture he recalled
Of that day when he was young.

Trance-formed now by the memory
His voice was close to tears
But the story he was telling
Was falling on deaf ears.

There was giggling and nudging
And lots of 'sssh – he'll hear'
For it was a trick, a game they played
Grown crueller with each year.

'Poor old Grandad' they tittered
As they one by one withdrew
'He's told it all so often
He now believes it's true.'

Young rabbits need fresh carrots
And his had long grown stale
So they left the old campaigner
Imprisoned in his tale.

Petrified by memories
Haunting ever strong
Encased in a block of time
Eighteen inches long.
* * *
Alone in a field in Devon
An old rabbit is sitting, talking,
When out of the wood, at the edge
of the world,
A man with a gun comes walking.

ROGER McGOUGH

AFTER READING

1 Choose three words which describe the character of Grandad.

2 What is the young rabbits' attitude to Grandad?

3 Why do you think Roger McGough has made the rabbit older, looking back on the event?

COMPARE

Discussion

1   Which of the main facts from the *Daily Telegraph* newspaper story has Roger McGough kept in his version?

2   What are the main changes he has made in retelling the story?

3   What are the advantages of telling the story in a poem rather than a newspaper – what freedom does it allow the writer? What are the advantages of reporting the story in a newspaper?

4   Look back at the dictionary definition of the word 'legend', what ingredients are there in Roger McGough's poem which make the rabbit story a legend?

Assignments

1   Reread the newspaper report, then retell the story in your own poem, this time from the point of view of Michael Hooper, the machine operator.

2   Look through today's newspaper and choose a story which appeals to you. Write the story in a different form as Roger McGough has done. You could write it as a diary account, or as a letter, or an interview. After redrafting, present the two versions together, facing each other. How did rewriting the story in a different form alter your presentation of the facts?

WIDER READING

Legends and folk tales
Alan Garner, *A Bag of Moonshine*; Angela Carter, *The Virago Book of Fairy Tales* and *The Second Virago Book of Fairy Tales*; George Luis Borges, Silvana Ocampo and A Bioy Casares, *The Book of Fantasy*; Rosalind Kerven, *Earth Magic, Sky Magic: North American Indian Tales*; Duncan and Linda Williamson, *The Genie and the Fisherman: and Other Tales from the Travelling People*.

Ballads
Several anthologies of ballads are available. See also Walter de la Mare's collection, *Come Hither*, and W H Auden and J Garrett's *The Poet's Tongue*. Individual poets have specialised or experimented with the ballad form – for example, Robert Browning (especially *The Pied Piper of Hamelin*); Stevie Smith; William Wordsworth; Edgar Allan Poe; Thomas Hardy.

AFTER READING

1 From your reading, choose three folk tales or legends that you have enjoyed, and write introductions to them. You should say what the reader should look out for in the stories and language.

2 Compare two or three ballads by different writers, examining how they tell the stories, and how they use language.

FIGHT FOR YOUR RIGHTS

Children in Victorian times were told that they should be seen and not heard. Many adults still believe that children should listen to their elders and do as they are told.
- *When is it important to argue your case, and when is it best to remain silent?*
- *What ways of speaking command the attention and the respect of an audience?*

HAPPIEST DAYS?

■ In the following passages, three teenagers have little control over very important aspects of their lives.

READING SKILLS
Seeking information
Summarising
Developing personal response

Oliver Twist

The room in which the boys were fed was a large stone hall, with a copper at one end, out of which the master, dressed in an apron for the purpose, and assisted by one or two women, ladled the gruel at meal-times; of which composition each boy had one porringer, and no more – except on festive occasions, and then he had two ounces and a quarter of bread besides. The bowls never wanted washing. The boys polished them with their spoons till they shone again; and when they had performed this operation (which never took very long, the spoons being nearly as large as the bowls), they would sit staring at the copper with such eager eyes as if they could have devoured the very bricks of which it was composed; employing themselves, meanwhile, in sucking their fingers most assiduously, with the view of catching up any stray splashes of gruel that might have been cast thereon. Boys have generally excellent appetites. Oliver Twist and his companions suffered the tortures of slow starvation for three months; at last they got so voracious and wild with hunger, that one boy, who was tall for this age, and hadn't been used to that sort of thing (for his father had kept a small cookshop), hinted darkly to his companion, that unless he had another basin of gruel *per diem*, he was afraid he might some night happen to eat the boy who slept next to him, who happened to be a weakly youth of tender age. He had a wild, hungry eye; and they implicitly believed him. A council was held; lots were cast who should walk up to the master after supper that evening, and ask for more; and it fell to Oliver Twist.

The evening arrived; the boys took their places. The master, in his cook's uniform, stationed himself at the copper; his pauper assistants ranged themselves behind him; the gruel was served out; and a long grace was said over the short commons. The gruel disappeared; the boys whispered to each other, and winked at Oliver, while his next neighbours nudged him. Child as he was, he was desperate with hunger, and reckless with misery. He rose from the table, and advancing to the master, basin and spoon in hand, said, somewhat alarmed at his own temerity:

'Please, sir, I want some more'.

The master was a fat, healthy man; but he turned very pale. He gazed in stupefied astonishment on the small rebel for some seconds, and then clung for support to the copper. The assistants were paralysed with wonder; the boys with fear.

'What!' said the master at length, in a faint voice.

'Please, sir,' replied Oliver, 'I want some more.'

The master aimed a blow at Oliver's head with the ladle, pinioned him in his arms, and shrieked aloud for the beadle.

The board were sitting in solemn conclave, when Mr Bumble rushed into the room in great excitement, and addressing the gentleman in the high chair, said,

'Mr Limbkins, I beg your pardon, sir! Oliver Twist has asked for more!' There was a general start. Horror was depicted on every countenance.

'For *more*!' said Mr Limbkins. 'Compose yourself, Bumble, and answer me distinctly. Do I understand that he asked for more, after he had eaten the supper allotted by the dietary?'

'He did, sir,' replied Bumble.

'That boy will be hung,' said the gentleman in the white waist-coat; 'I know that boy will be hung.'

Nobody controverted the prophetic gentleman's opinion. An animated discussion took place. Oliver was ordered into instant confinement; and a bill was next morning posted on the outside of the gate, offering a reward of five pounds to anybody who would take Oliver Twist off the hands of the parish. In other words, five pounds and Oliver Twist were offered to any man or woman who wanted an apprentice to any trade, business or calling.

CHARLES DICKENS

AFTER READING

1 How do you know that this story is set in the past?

2 What makes Oliver ask for more?

■ This novel is set in a village in Trinidad soon after the second World War. Tiger, a sixteen-year-old Indian boy, discovers that he is about to be married.

A Brighter Sun

TIGER didn't know anything about the wedding until his father told him. He didn't even know the girl. But he bowed to his parents' wishes. He was only sixteen years old and was not in the habit of attending Indian ceremonies in the village. But he knew a little about weddings, that Indians were married at an early age, and that after the ceremony friends and relatives would bring him gifts until he began to eat; only then would they stop the offerings.

Every night and every morning for a week close relatives came and rubbed him down to prepare his body for married life. On the morning of the wedding he bathed. They dressed him in the wedding gown and put a crown on his head. His father said, "Boy, dese people not so rich, so don't stayam too long to eat."

At the back of the bride's house a great tent of bamboo coconut branches had been erected. Five goats and six sheep had been slaughtered, an extravagance which could be afforded only at a time like this.

Tiger looked at everybody and everything with a tight feeling in his throat. He wished he knew more about what was going to happen to him.

As part of the ceremony he had to rub a red powder through the path in the middle of her head when a white sheet was thrown over them. As he did this he lifted the veil and looked at her face. She must have been about his age. She had black, sad eyes, long hair, undeveloped breasts.

"What you name?" he asked breathlessly.

"Urmilla," she whispered timidly.

Tiger didn't think that he would have to look at that face for the rest of his life. The whole affair had been arranged for him; he didn't have anything to do with it. He wondered if she could cook, but he didn't ask himself if she knew anything about what boys and girls did when they got married, because he didn't know either. He was aware of a painful exhilaration; painful because neither of them understood, exhilarating because it was something different in his monotonous life.

They offered him a cow and a hut in Barataria and two hundred dollars in cash, besides smaller things. He didn't know where Barataria was. He didn't know what to expect, or whether he should wait for more gifts before beginning the feast. And then on a sudden impulse – perhaps it was fear, uncertainty – he took up a piece of *meetai* and bit it. That ended the offerings.

Afterwards his father caught him alone for a minute and

hissed, "Yuh fool! Could have gettam plenty more thing! Yuh eatam too quick, stupid boy!".

But it didn't matter to Tiger. Vaguely, like morning mist, he found himself wondering what life was going to be like.

As was the custom, the bride had to spend three days at his home, then they would spend three days at her family's. After that they could go and live in their own house.

When Tiger had handed Urmilla over to his mother, all the boys and girls from the neighbourhood came up and started to call out to him.

"Tiger! So yuh married now!"

"Yuh is a big man now, boy!"

Some of the older folk drove them away, but Tiger would have liked them to come. He was familiar with them, he could make jokes and talk. But now he was a man. He would have to learn to be a man, he would have to forget his friends. After all, he thought, they still little children!

In the next three days his mind was in turmoil. He went out into the canefields where he had toiled with his father and brothers. Wind blew strongly here: he liked to lift his head and smell burned cane. What had life been for him? Days in the fields, evenings playing with other children, roti and *aloo* in the night. Sometimes they sang songs. His father had a drum, and when it was Saturday night the neighbours came and they drank and sang. And now all that was gone. He felt a tremendous responsibility falling on his shoulders. He tried not to think about it.

SAMUEL SELVON

AFTER READING

1 Make a list of the three things that you find most interesting and/or surprising about Tiger's wedding. Discuss your list with your partner.

2 What do you learn about Tiger's wedding ceremony? In what ways is it similar to or different from the wedding ceremonies that you are familiar with?

■ Written by a fourteen-year-old schoolboy, this article describes the problems he faces in and out of school.

The Happiest Days of my Life?

Today's schoolkids live under a cloud of potential violence. A 14-year-old at a London suburban comprehensive has written this first-hand account.

The hulking boy demanded: "Giz your trainers,". One of his minions backed him up: "Yeah, or we'll do you in." My mind raced to find a way to outwit the large gang of adolescents who had surrounded me. This may not sound like a difficult task. But for some reason my powers of negotiation had disappeared. "I can't," I blurted out. "They're not mine."

Too late it hit me that I had just admitted to being arguably the worst thing in the eyes of the average 12-year-old: the sort of kid who wore his brother's cast-off clothes – what is known in comprehensive school slang as a "tramp".

The leader of the group was on to it immediately. "What are you then, a tramp?" he inquired. Once again my mind searched for a fitting answer, and once again I could do no better than a short "Yeah, that's right." This appeared to stun them for a moment. But then one of them had a brainstorm. He decided to pull a knife on me. "What's that?" I asked, looking at the half-inch blade he wielded between two fingers.

"It's a knife," he said aggressively. "Oh," I said, trying not to sound too sarcastic or to laugh. Then suddenly it was all over. They lost interest in me and left to taunt another innocent pupil or to steal his ball. Later I found out that it had simply been because I had been a new kid arriving from another school at the beginning of the second year.

That was over a year ago and the problem of being new is gone – but not the problem of bullying. Don't get me wrong. I go to a good comprehensive school in a nice London suburb. But outside the classroom, life is a battle, even if it isn't one inside. Grange Hill on BBC1 is quite realistic about school life. It's not escapist like The Wonder Years. But even Grange Hill underestimates the amount of smoking, drinking, the drugs and the violence. And there's too much good guy stuff – hard kids giving cigarettes to small kids, things like that. As one of my older brothers put it after attending the same school: "You live under a permanent cloud of potential violence, and it leaves its mark."

When you arrive at your secondary school at 11 everyone is almost the same. Hardly anyone smokes or drinks and you all watch Top Of The Pops. That's something they deny later, when they've turned into a Raver or a Metaller. "I was never like that, I was always like this," they say. But they were. And the first step to changing is based on the type of music you like.

Roughly speaking there are two groups of people in school: people who are normal and people who aren't. The normal ones are the ones who don't look normal to adults. The abnormal ones are kids who aren't real. They're programmed by their parents and they have no social life. The highlight of their day is a double homework in biology. These are the people who spend their free time bettering themselves for their parents. They are sometimes called "boffins" or "sad cases". In my other brother's school they were called "stretch-heads". These people are difficult to talk to in a friendly, social way, and only those with siblings can handle the most simple social tasks. They all talk down to you, get straight As and are the teacher's pet. But they probably have the most problems and suffer most from the bullies of the school. It's not hard to get angry at them and their patronising or unusual ways. But you still have to feel sorry for them.

There is another group of kids who get called boffins – but only by the less intelligent creatures that lurk around the boys' toilets with a packet of 20 Silk Cut. This other type of boffin never fitted into the abnormal section. They are just the intelligent kids who do well. You can talk to them and see them out of school.

Most of these kids in Boffin Section B are now my friends. You see, they go through a change, often around the middle of the second year. They grow their hair and get hard. Often they end up as Metallers, though occasionally they become Ravers. I will explain these categories later.

By the time they are my age – 14 – most normal kids have formed into groups which are almost totally music-orientated unless they are sport-orientated or, in some schools, social-class-orientated. I expect that different schools in different parts of the country use different slang. New groups and slang are emerging all the time. There aren't many kids who are only into sport in my school. Most are at least slightly music-orientated, but not quite all. At our school the main groups are Ravers, Metallers, Fashion Victims and, of course, Trevs and Sharons, which even adults have heard about. You can always spot a Sharon Patrol. They're the girls with bobbled out hair, big loop earrings and pink lipstick. Trevs – private school kids call them Kevs – wear shiny tracksuits out of school and in school too – if they come. They are called Trevs because they act or talk stupidly, and these names are meant to sound common or stupid.

Sharons like bands with no talent, 10 minutes of fame types like Bros, Jason Donovan, New Kids on the Block, Take That and East 17 – whoever happens to be in at the time. It is considered sad for boys to like pop, so most of this type are girls – Sharons, not Trevs. Their folders are decorated with pictures of this week's Top Of The Pops celebrity. Ravers don't like anything that goes into the charts. The moment it does it becomes pop and they abandon it. Rave has the most followers, even more than rock and metal.

Ravers like Hard Core, they take rap music, TV commercial jingles (not the lyrics) and mix it. They listen to pirate radio and go to raves where they do drugs ranging from the simple joint through to the most common fashion drug, Ecstasy, otherwise known as Es. Some Ravers don't mind how they dress, others wear designer label clothes like the fashion victims, labels like Chippie or Chevignon. The difference is that Ravers enjoy raving. Fashion

Victims don't actually like what they do, they do it to be fashionable.

Metallers (pronounced metlars) are called that because they like heavy metal music. They wear torn jeans and denim or leather jackets with "Metalice" or "Iron Maiden" written on the back in peeling letters. They wear mainly black and have long hair unless their school makes them get it cut. Ours doesn't. The odd one of them will like Indy bands: The Cure, Sheep on Drugs.

The most popular of the Indy bands with the Metallers is Nirvana, as it can be classified as Metal or Indy because of how it sounds.

There are a few groups of people left which are not very popular at my school and scarcely found, one of them being Indy-followers or Goths. Indy-followers dress differently to Metallers, more extreme with crustie hair, crustie clothes and – often – rich parents. Goths, or Gothics, dress even more extreme than that. They wear all black clothes and white make-up with red lips, as much as they can get away with at school but more out of school. Goths emerged from Indy-followers who emerged from Metallers, just as Hip-Hop and Hard Core emerged from Ravers. A Crustie, also rare, is a variety of Goth or Indy-follower who wears huge sweaters with holes in them. He/she is often a rich kid rebelling against their parents.

The other small group at our school is Raggas – black kids who aren't sporty, boffins or fitting into the other categories. These are the kids who like what they like, have an attitude and a haircut to prove it. The easiest place to find them when they're not at school – which is often – is at a fairground. You can see them holding smaller kids up against the Street-Fighter arcade machine demanding money. If you show them you're not going to give them anything, but without being rude, they'll most likely leave you alone.

There are still a lot of people at school who don't fall into any particular group and like different music of their own choice: reggae, classical, or bits of everything. They don't dress like a group either. I used to be thought of as a bit of a boffin until I grew my hair and started dressing all in black. Then I was called a tramp but only by the opposing groups. Let me explain.

There is a constant war between Metallers and Ravers. Ravers call the Metallers "tramps" because of their long hair and ripped jeans. In my experience a lot of Metallers are still on the verge of being boffins, or their parents are quite rich. Maybe they think that acting like this is a rebellion against their parents and against the way they are treated in school. Ravers don't seem to have such an expensive lifestyle or get such good marks. Whether this means that rave appeals to less intelligent people or that ravers just don't care about their work, I don't know.

Like I said before, there is a lot of violence. Sometimes it is directed against other schools, if a girl's been cussed and she knows enough people or the right people. That can end up in a fight, usually in a park. Some people bring screwdrivers or knives and kids can get hurt. When my brother was still at the school one kid brought a shotgun.

Other times the violence is directed against private school kids who are too sheltered to be able to look after themselves – even the ones who think they're hard. Third years go off to humiliate or beat up private school fifth years on the bus. A lot of violence takes places on buses, much more than on the Tube. That's where my latest trouble has come from.

A kid I used to be friends with turned against me after being told that I'd been insulting him. This was untrue, but within a week, I was beaten up in a phone box by friends of the boy in question, while the friend I was with was held against a wall. One of the attackers was from my school and in the fifth year. He was with his younger brother, who was my age but at another school. I got away with only a cut lip and a bruised ego.

This kind of thing went on for a few weeks and was quite difficult to avoid as these kids used to hang around the station I use to go to school. None of my friends who use the same station could really do anything to help because a lot of older teenagers hang out there. It is a kind of Station Mafia. My older brothers said they couldn't interfere because that would only makes things worse. They were right. If I got back-up, the mafia would get more back-up and someone would end up stabbed. So I had to live with it.

Suddenly it seemed to sort itself out and I thought it was all over. But then I started getting phone calls at anything from 11pm to 3am. No one said anything – they just hung up. It went on until my mother told a girl who goes to our school and is friendly with the Station Mafia that she'd had a special trace put on incoming calls.

I found out who was behind it: my ex-friend – let's call him Dick – who was a godson of the Station Mafia. Within a day of finding out this information I was told I was to have a fight with him. I was considered the winner of the first fight after I head-butted him and made his nose bleed. So they organised a second one after he ran a smear campaign, telling my friends individually that I'd been cussing them too. He pulled my hair until an old lady stopped the fight. Everyone said he was the winner, but the next week he got a bigger kid in our year to head-butt me in the face instead of trying it himself.

I still get hassled at school, by kids he's set on me. Why don't my parents complain? Well, they did talk to the school, but the teachers have enough problems with what goes on during schooltime without taking on problems outside.

So take it from me: whatever anyone else may say or think, there's a lot of pain in these adolescent years, and no one misses out on it. It's really not fair to tell your children that these are the best years of their lives: it doesn't give them a lot to look forward to. Anyone who was ever nostalgic about childhood was evidently never a child.

THE GUARDIAN

AFTER READING

1 Is this what school life is like for you? In what ways is the writer's lifestyle similar to yours, and how does it differ?

COMPARE

Discussion

1 Choose three key words to describe the problems that Oliver faces, three more to describe the problems that Tiger faces, and three to describe the schoolboy's problems. Write these down and, with your partner, say why you think these words sum up each of the boy's difficulties.

2 Parents and guardians play different roles in these passages. Oliver, an orphan, is completely powerless under the authority of the beadle. Tiger's parents have the authority to arrange his marriage without consulting him, but the schoolboy's parents don't have the power to stop him being bullied. In pairs or small groups, discuss what control you think parents should have over their children. Be prepared to share your ideas with the whole class.

Assignments

1 What advice would you give to Oliver, Tiger or the author of 'The Happiest Days of my Life?' When you have made some notes, write your advice down in the form of a letter.

2 Make a list of the different groups in your school, then write a definition of what it means to be a member of that group. (Look again at 'The Happiest Days of my Life?' to see what sort of information the author includes in his definitions). Set out your list of groups in dictionary form and illustrate it.

3 Write your own 'Good Parents' Guide'. This should contain an introduction, stating who the guide is aimed at and why it is important that it is read, together with ten key points of advice for prospective parents. Make sure that each point is backed up by examples of how good parents should behave.

4 "Whatever anyone else may say or think, there's a lot of pain in these adolescent years and no one misses out on it. It's not really fair to tell your children that these are the best years of their lives: it doesn't give them a lot to look forward to."
Do you agree with this statement? Make some notes on your views on being an adolescent. Use these to write an essay on this subject to inform adults (who quickly forget) what it is really like to be your age.

SPEAK YOUR MIND

■ The people who make the next three speeches gain power and influence through their use of language.

JULIUS CAESAR

Caesar has been assassinated by Brutus, one of his most trusted friends, and several senators. A crowd has gathered at the scene of the assassination. Brutus has explained to the crowd why he felt that he had to kill Caesar; he believes that he has explained his side of the case so well that he can afford to let Mark Antony, Caesar's closest ally, give Caesar's funeral oration. Mark Antony uses his speech to turn the crowd against Brutus and the other assassins.

ANTONY   Friends, Romans, countrymen, lend me your ears.
I come to bury Caesar, not to praise him.
The evil that men do lives after them,
The good is oft interred with their bones.
So let it be with Caesar. The noble Brutus
Hath told you Caesar was ambitious.
If it were so, it was a grievous fault
And grievously hath Caesar answered it.
Here, under leave of Brutus and the rest,
(For Brutus is an honourable man,
So are they all – all honourable men)
Come I to speak in Caesar's funeral.
He was my friend, faithful and just to me,
But Brutus says he was ambitious,
And Brutus is an honourable man.
He hath brought many captives home to Rome,
Whose ransoms did the general coffers fill.
Did this in Caesar seem ambitious?
When the poor have cried, Caesar hath wept.
Ambition should be made of sterner stuff.
Yet Brutus says he was ambitious,
And Brutus is an honourable man.
You all did see that on the Lupercal
I thrice presented him a kingly crown,
Which he did thrice refuse. Was this ambition?
Yet Brutus says he was ambitious,
And sure he is an honourable man.
I speak not to disprove what Brutus spoke,
But here I am to speak what I do know.
You all did love him once, not without cause.

What cause witholds you then to mourn for him?
O judgment, thou art fled to brutish beasts.
And men have lost their reason. Bear with me.
My heart is in the coffin there with Caesar,
And I must pause till it come back to me.

1st PLEBIAN   Methinks there is much reason in his sayings.

2nd PLEBIAN   If thou consider rightly of the matter,
Caesar has had great wrong.

3rd PLEBIAN   Has he, masters?
I fear there will a worse come in his place.

4th PLEBIAN   Marked ye his words? He would not take the crown;
Therefore 'tis certain he was not ambitious.

1st PLEBIAN   If it be found so, some will dear abide it.

2nd PLEBIAN   Poor soul! His eyes are red as fire with weeping.

3rd PLEBIAN   There's not a nobler man in Rome than Antony.

4th PLEBIAN   Now mark him, he begins again to speak.

ANTONY   But yesterday the word of Caesar might
Have stood against the world. Now lies he there,
And none so poor to do him reverence.
O masters, if I were disposed to stir
Your hearts and minds to mutiny and rage
I should do Brutus wrong, and Cassius wrong,
Who you all know are honourable men.
I will not do them wrong. I rather choose
To wrong the dead, to wrong myself and you,
Than I will wrong such honourable men.
But here's a parchment with the seal of Caesar.
I found it in his closet – 'tis his will.
Let but the commons hear this testament,
Which, pardon me, I do not mean to read,
And they would go and kiss dead Caesar's wounds,
And dip their napkins in his sacred blood,
Yea, beg a hair of him for memory,
And dying, mention it within their wills,
Bequeathing it as a rich legacy
Unto their issue.

4th PLEBIAN   We'll hear the will! Read it Mark Antony.

ALL   The will, the will! We will hear Caesar's will.

ANTONY   Have patience gentle friends, I must not read it.
It is not meet you know how Caesar loved you.
You are not wood, you are not stones, but men,
And being men, hearing the will of Caesar,

It will inflame you, it will make you mad.
'Tis good you know not that you are his heirs,
For if you should, O what would come of it!

4 PLEBIAN   Read the will! We'll hear it Antony.
You shall read us the will, Caesar's will!

ANTONY   Will you be patient? Will you stay awhile?
I have o'ershot myself to tell you of it.
I fear I wrong the honourable men
Whose daggers have stabbed Caesar; I do fear it.

4th PLEBIAN   They were traitors. Honourable men!

ALL   The will! The testament!

2nd PLEBIAN   They were villains, murderers!
The will, read the will!

ANTONY   You will compel me then to read the will?
Then make a ring about the corpse of Caesar,
And let me show you him that made the will.
Shall I descend? And will you give me leave?

ALL   Come down.

2nd PLEBIAN   Descend

3rd PLEBIAN   You shall have leave. *[ANTONY comes down]*

4th PLEBIAN   A ring, stand round!

1st PLEBIAN   Stand from the hearse, stand from the body.

2nd PLEBIAN   Room for Antony, most noble Antony.

ANTONY   Nay, press not so upon me. Stand far off.

SEVERAL PLEBIANS   Stand back. Room! Bear back!

ANTONY   If you have tears, prepare to shed them now.
You all do know this mantle. I remember
The first time ever Caesar put it on -
'Twas on a summer's evening in his tent,
That day he overcame the Nervii.
Look, in this place ran Cassius' dagger through;
See what a rent the envious Casca made.
Through this the well-beloved Brutus stabbed,
And as he plucked his cursed steel away
Mark how the blood of Caesar followed it,
As rushing out of doors, to be resolved
If Brutus so unkindly knocked or no,
For Brutus, as you know, was Caesar's angel.
Judge, O you gods, how dearly Caesar loved him.
This was the most unkindest cut of all,
For when the noble Caesar saw him stab,

Ingratitude, more strong than traitors' arms,
Quite vanquished him. Then burst his mighty heart,
And in his mantle muffling up his face,
Even at the base of Pompey's statua,
Which all the while ran blood, great Caesar fell.
O what a fall was there, my countrymen!
Then I, and you, and all of us fell down
Whilst bloody treason flourished over us.
O now you weep, and I perceive you feel
The dint of pity. These are gracious drops.
Kind souls! What, weep you when you but behold
Our Caesar's vesture wounded? Look you here,
Here is himself, marred as you see with traitors.

1st PLEBIAN   O piteous spectacle!

2nd PLEBIAN   O noble Caesar!

3rd PLEBIAN   O woeful day!

4th PLEBIAN   O traitors, villains!

1st PLEBIAN   O most bloody sight!

2nd PLEBIAN   We will be revenged.

WILLIAM SHAKESPEARE

AFTER READING

1 What arguments does Mark Antony use to turn the crowd against Brutus and the other assassins?

2 Look up the word 'irony' in the dictionary. Mark Antony uses irony in this speech to turn the crowd against Brutus. How does he do it?

■ Born to parents who were slaves, Sojourner Truth was, at the age of nine, taken from her parents and sold at a slave auction. Once freed, she became an activist and spoke out against the double discrimination of racism and sexism that black women faced. Her famous speech is here adapted into a poem.

Ain't I a Woman?

That man over there say
a woman needs to be helped into carriages
and lifted over ditches
and to have the best place everywhere.
Nobody ever helped me into carriages
or over mud puddles
or gives me a best place...

Ain't I a woman?
Look at me
Look at my arm!
I have plowed and planted
and gathered into barns
and no man could head me...
And ain't I a woman?
I could work as much
and eat as much as a man –
when I could get to it –
and bear the lash as well

and ain't I a woman?
I have born thirteen children
and seen most all sold into slavery
and when I cried out a mother's grief
none but Jesus heard me...
and ain't I a woman?
That little man in black there say
a woman can't have as much rights as a man
cause Christ wasn't a woman.
Where did your Christ come from?
From God and a woman!
Man had nothing to do with him!
If the first woman God ever made
was strong enough to turn the world
upside down, all alone
together women ought to be able to turn it
rightside up again.

adapted by ERLENE STETSON

AFTER READING

1 What arguments does Sojourner Truth use to advance her belief that women should be given the same rights as men?

2 What emotions do you feel when you read this speech?

I have a dream

■ Martin Luther King made this speech to a crowd of 200,000 people in Washington in 1963 at the height of the Black Civil Rights movement

I say to you today, my friends, that in spite of the difficulties and frustrations of the moment I still have a dream. I have a dream that one day this nation will rise up and live out the true meaning of its creed: 'We hold these truths to be self-evident: that all men are created equal.'

I have a dream that one day on the red hills of Georgia the sons of former slaves and the sons of former slave-owners will be able to sit down together at the table of brotherhood.

I have a dream that one day even the state of Mississippi will be transformed into an oasis of freedom and justice.

I have a dream that my four little children will one day live in a nation where they will not be judged by the color of their skin, but by the content of their character.

This will be the day when all of God's children will be able to sing with new meaning 'My country 'tis of thee let freedom ring.'

And if America is to be a great nation, this must become true. So let freedom ring from the prodigious hilltops of New Hampshire. Let freedom ring from the mighty mountains of New York. But not only that. Let freedom ring from every hill and molehill of Mississippi.

When we let freedom ring from every town and every hamlet, from every state and every city, we will be able to speed up that day when all God's children, black men and white men, Jews and Gentiles, Protestant and Catholics, will be able to join hands and sing in the words of that old Negro spiritual, 'Free at last! Free at last! Thank God almighty, we are free at last.'

MARTIN LUTHER KING

AFTER READING

1 What is Martin Luther King's dream of the America that he wants to see created?

COMPARE

Discussion

1　Working in groups of four or five prepare a reading of one of the speeches. Every group member should take a part. You will need to decide how the lines should be said, what actions to make as you talk and what the reaction of the crowd might be to what you are saying. When you have practised, perform your version of the speech to the rest of the class. You will then have the opportunity to compare different groups' interpretations of the different speeches.

2　What do you learn about each of the speakers from what they say in their speeches?

3　Look again at two of the three speeches and make a list of key words and phrases in it. Compare your list with someone else's, and discuss why you think these words and phrases are important.

4　Which speech do you think is the most effective and why?

Assignments

1   Look again at the key words and phrases that you have already identified in one of the speeches. Speakers use certain techniques to convince audiences of their case. One of these is repetition (stating the same word, or phrase or idea repeatedly, in order to make it stick in the listeners' minds). Other common techniques are:

- asking rhetorical questions
- using language which touches the listeners' emotions
- building up to a climax
- anticipating the arguments that the other side might put forward, and answering them in your speech (getting your word in first!)

Take one of the speeches and make notes on the rhetorical devices that the speaker uses to argue his case powerfully. Use your notes to write a commentary on the speech.

2   Remembering all that you have learned about rhetoric, prepare a speech on a subject that you feel strongly about. When planning your speech, make sure that you:

- know what you want to say
- have several key points that you want to get across
- decide which order you want to put your arguments in

When you have planned and practised your speech, deliver it to an audience. Remember that it is much more effective if you talk from notes rather than reading all of your speech.

3   Collect leaflets that promote a cause or a product (e.g. Body Shop, estate agents, campaign leaflets). Write about how language is used to persuade the reader that this product or cause is genuine or worthy. Pay particular attention to the techniques of language that are used.

WIDER READING

Fiction
Many novelists speak powerfully through the characters they create in their novels.

Robert Leeson, *It's My Life*; Charlotte Brontë, *Jane Eyre*; Harper Lee, *To Kill a Mockingbird*; Richard Wright, *Black Boy*; J.D. Salinger, *The Catcher In The Rye*; Lynne Reid Banks, *The Writing on The Wall*.

Poetry
Poets often express their anger or discontent with the way things are through their poetry. The following anthologies are recommended.

Simon Fuller (ed), *The Poetry of Protest*: *Yesterday Today Tomorrow* (NATE publication). The poetry of Wilfred Owen, Siegfried Sassoon and the other poets of the first World War – *War Poems* by Christopher Martin (Collins Educational).

AFTER READING

1 Write your own story in which a character eventually speaks out against an injustice.

2 Do you agree that the novelist or poet had a good cause to speak out about?

UNEXPLAINED MYSTERIES

Although science is able to explain much of what happens in the world, there are some mysteries which still baffle us today.
- *Which of these mysteries do you believe in: unidentified flying objects (UFOs), the Loch Ness Monster, ghosts, the Abominable Snowman?*
- *Do you dismiss these things as superstitious nonsense, or do you believe that there may be other forms of life out there somewhere, watching and waiting...?*

BELIEVE IT OR NOT?

■ *The Unexplained* is a magazine for people interested in mysterious phenomena. This questionnaire comes from the magazine – it is supposed to help you work out your own viewpoint on certain issues.

READING SKILLS

Seeking information

ARE YOU PSYCHICALLY AWARE?

Believer or sceptic, there's no reason why you shouldn't test your own psychic powers. And you're not alone: people the world over – famous names among them – have their own paranormal tales to tell.

Here are 10 questions to help you discover if you are receptive to the idea of unexplained phenomena. Simply choose (a), (b) or (c) for each question to find our how ready you are to open up to The Unexplained.

Q1
Complex operations are sometimes carried out by 'psychic surgeons'. Do you think these surgeons are:

(a) Dangerous criminals who should be locked up?
(b) Harmless faith healers?
(c) Blessed with powers that may be of great benefit to mankind?

Q2
Voodoo religion is full of references to zombies. Are they:

(a) Corpses who are turned into mindless slaves by voodoo sorcerers?
(b) Totally fictional?
(c) Victims of hypnosis?

Q3

Everybody has a theory about the origin of UFOs. Do you think they are:

(a) Alien spacecraft from distant planets?
(b) Figments of the imagination?
(c) Aircraft, or natural phenomena?

Q4

What do you make of stories of people who claim to have levitated?

(a) I'd only believe it if I saw it with my own eyes.
(b) Some people have the ability to defy the force of gravity and rise into the air.
(c) It's nothing more than a stage trick.

Q5

If someone put a curse on you and you subsequently found yourself suffering from an illness, would you:

(a) Laugh it off as mere superstition?
(b) Seek some form of protection – religious, psychic or otherwise?
(c) Regard the illness as psychosomatic?

Q6

Are photographs of 'ghosts':

(a) Spirits of the departed?
(b) Projections of the unconscious mind?
(c) All fakes, designed to fool the gullible?

Q7

What do you make of the claims of fakirs who say they can survive without food or water for long periods of time?

(a) Absolute nonsense.
(b) It may be possible.
(c) Nothing is beyond the power of the human mind.

Q8

People claim that objects can be moved from one place to another, without physical means. Is this:

(a) 'Psychokinesis' – the effect of mind over matter?
(b) Totally impossible?
(c) An unexplained scientific phenomenon?

Q9

Do you think that spontaneous human combustion is:

(a) A subject deserving investigation?
(b) A very real and frightening prospect?
(c) A myth created by the media?

Q10

Are out-of-body experiences an indication of:

(a) The separation of mind and body?
(b) Hallucination as a result of a frail physical condition?
(c) A glimpse into another dimension – that of life after death?

Now turn the page and find out how receptive you are towards The Unexplained...

THE UNEXPLAINED QUIZ

How did you score?

	(a)		(b)		(c)	
1.	1 point		3 pts		5 pts	
2.	5		1		3	
3.	5		3		1	
4.	3		5		1	
5.	1		5		3	
6.	5		3		1	
7.	1		3		5	
8.	5		1		3	
9.	3		5		1	
10.	3		1		5	

How ready are you to open up?

If you scored between 10 and 19:
You tend to be sceptical towards the paranormal and always require scientific evidence – such as that regularly provided in *The Unexplained* – before accepting.

If you scored between 20 and 30:
You are reluctant to dismiss paranormal phenomena out of hand, and like to draw your own conclusions. *The Unexplained* will provide you with precisely this opportunity.

If you scored between 31 and 50:
You never automatically dismiss accounts of strange but supposedly true phenomena or bizarre events, so you're sure to find *The Unexplained* fascinating reading.

AFTER READING

1 Before looking at the answer panel, think a bit more about the questionnaire: is there a pattern to the way it has been written? For example, can you work out which answers – (a), (b) or (c) – you think are most likely to be ticked by 'believers'?

2 Now look at the answer panel to see if your prediction was right.

Discussion

1 In pairs, discuss how well the questionnaire works.

2 What other questions might you have asked if you had compiled the questionnaire?

Assignments

You have been asked to undertake some market research to find out people's views on unexplained mysteries, before a new magazine series on the subject is produced. You need much more detailed results than were revealed by the questionnaire. How would you devise another questionnaire or information-gathering method which would give fuller answers to the following questions?

- Do more people believe in UFOs than in ghosts?
- Are young people more likely than older people to be open-minded about UFOs?
- What percentage of teenagers claim to have 'seen' a ghost?
- Which of the following do people believe in most and least strongly: ghosts, UFOs, the Loch Ness Monster, levitation?

BIGFOOT FACT AND FICTION

■ For hundreds of years there have been reported sightings of the 'Abominable Snowman', a huge creature said to lurk in the Himalayan Mountains. But 'Bigfoot' or 'Sasquatch' has also been spotted in other parts of the world. Read this account of Sasquatch sightings; then read the story by Tim Crawley based on the same reports.

SASQUATCH SIGHTINGS

During a salmon run in the Nooksack River near Marietta, Washington, in mid-September 1967, several local anglers reported Sasquatch sightings.

Early one morning Harold James was going upriver about 15 feet from shore when he became aware of a strong wet-animal odour that was vaguely familiar. Looking across a bog, he saw something sitting on a stump; and when it rose and walked away, he saw that it was a dark creature twice the size of a man.

That afternoon a married couple who were also fishing saw a creature standing in the river about 200 yards away. Up to its knees in water, it stood about eight feet tall and was slightly stooped. Its body was black, its face flat, and it had no neck. As the couple watched, the creature bent down and submerged. Tracks found on a sandbar showed a five-toed foot 13 ½ inches long and a stride measuring 45 inches.

Drifting his gill net down a channel one night, Johnny Green discovered that it was disappearing over the edge of his boat. The powerful spotlight Green wore on his head played on a big hairy beast standing in the water, pulling at the net. Green shouted to his friends, Reynold James and Randy Kinley, who came down and shone more lights upon the creature. It let go of the net and lumbered away on the shore. (John Green, *The Sasquatch File*, p.36)

Roger Patterson, a Bigfoot buff for many years, set up camp at the bottom of Bluff Creek Valley, in northern California, in October 1967 with the intention of filming fresh tracks with his 16mm movie camera.

Accompanied by his colleague Bob Gimlin, Patterson

made daily horseback patrols of sandbars on which tracks had previously been seen. One day the men rounded a bend and saw a large, dark animal squatting on the bank at the far side of the creek. The horses reared at the sight and Patterson fell. As he scrambled to his feet he frantically clawed open his saddle bag to get out the movie camera, but by then the creature was walking away. Patterson ran after it, then stopped and filmed from a distance of about 80 feet.

He managed to shoot a few clear frames that show a heavily built creature, about seven feet tall and three feet across the shoulders, covered with black hair. It strides smoothly, with its knees bent. As it turns to look at Patterson, it reveals large, drooping breasts. The face is flat and hairy, with heavy brow ridges. The head is peaked at the back and sits right on the shoulders.

The creature – she – went off into the brush, leaving footprints 14½ inches long. Patterson and Gimlin made two crisp casts and several still photographs of the tracks. According to one investigator, John Green, analysis of the material revealed no evidence of fraud. (John Green, *On the Track of the Sasquatch*, pp.51-57, and *The Sasquatch File*, p.39)

A similar encounter unnerved Mrs Louise Baxter of Skamania, Washington, on August 19, 1970. Driving in the vicinity of the Beacon Rock trailer park, Mrs Baxter began to suspect that she had a flat tyre, and so she got out of her car to check:

'I kicked the tyre, which was okay, and then bent over to see if possibly something was stuck under the fender to make the noise.

I suddenly felt as if I was being watched and without straightening up I looked toward the wooden area beside the road and looked straight into the face of the biggest creature I have ever seen except the one the time nearly a year before.

The creature was coconut brown and shaggy and dirty-looking... The mouth was partly open and I saw a row of large square white teeth. The head was big and seemed to set right onto the shoulders. The ears were not visible due to the long hair about the head. It seemed the hair was about two inches long on its head.

It had a jutted chin and receding forehead. The nose and upper lip were less hairy and the nose was wide with big nostrils.

The eyes were the most outstanding as they were amber colour and seemed to glow like an animal's eyes at night when car lights catch them.

It seemed contented there and seemed to be eating as the left fist was up toward the mouth as though it had something in it.

I screamed or hollered but whether I made any noise I can't tell I was so terrified. I know it didn't move while I looked. I don't remember how I got back in the car or how I started it. As I pulled out I could see it still standing there, all 10 or 12 feet of him.' (John Green, *The Sasquatch File*, p.53)

MYSTERIES OF THE UNEXPLAINED, READER'S DIGEST 1982

AFTER READING

1 What do the two Sasquatch sightings have in common?

2 Which eyewitness do you find most reliable or believable, and why?

3 How has the author of these accounts tried to make them seem factual?

Put Your Best Bigfoot Forward

Wayne slumped down into a pile of leaves with a muffled groan. Elmer squatted down on his haunches.

"Well that was a blast! I can see the headlines now, 'Bigfoot exists – startling new pictures!'" Wayne moved his shoulders about inside his Acme Fancy Dress Sasquatch suit. He began to struggle with the zip that held the head on to the padded shoulders of the Bigfoot outfit. Elmer just stared at the fallen leaves between his feet. He picked one up gently between his leathery fingers and examined it.

"Did you see the faces of those campers, Elmer? When we ran through their clearing as they were eating their barbecue?"

Elmer stared at Wayne. Through his Sasquatch mask, his eyes looked huge brown and thoughtful. Elmer sighed. It sounded like, "Uffffffffah!", the sound something heavy would make if dropped into a pile of dry leaves.

"Did you see their faces? That old lady who swallowed her false teeth and turned blue when she saw not one but two Bigfoot, er Bigfeet, run through her campsite!" Wayne laughed, rolling on his back slapping his sides. Elmer gently and carefully straightened a young tree that had been squashed by a fallen branch and said nothing.

"Ever the strong silent type, eh Elmer?" Wayne began to struggle again with the zipper holding on the head of his costume. His eyes appeared and disappeared in the eye holes as he twisted his head around inside.

"I can't see a thing. It's starting to get hot in here too. I'll smell like a real Sasquatch soon, not that there is such a thing." Elmer leant slowly forward and sniffed four long slow sniffs. "Snirfff, snoorfff, snarrrfff, snurrrfff," then he shook his head sadly.

"Very funny Elmer. You don't smell so good yourself. I tell you what though, I thought you were brilliant, the way you went crashing through those bushes at the edge of that camp site and then suddenly dropped down from that tree branch. I don't know how you did that. I didn't realise how fit you are. That's some trick that, disappearing into the bushes then seconds later coming down out of that tree. Wowee! Know what I mean?"

Wayne pushed Elmer firmly away as he tried to pick something out of his fake nylon fur.

"Do you know, Elmer, I think you might be taking all this too seriously. Ever since you put that Sasquatch outfit on, you've been behaving strangely. There are places you can sniff and places you can't. And that, get off, is one of those you can't."

"Urrrgh!" said Elmer and covered the top of his head with his long arms.

"Look Elmer, enough is enough! I've enjoyed frightening those campers and I shall enjoy even more seeing those photographs in the national papers but ...... Look, help me off with the head of this suit." Wayne began to wrench at the head of the suit again. There was a sudden snap.

"Shoot! Well that's done it!" Wayne held the snapped-off zipper tag between the baggy fingertips of his Sasquatch gloves. "I don't suppose you've got any scissors in your pockets... oh, of course you've got no pockets in there have you? Of course not, they'll be in your jeans back in the pick-up truck."

Elmer picked up a handful of leaves and threw them at Wayne.

"Bleugh! Coffewagggh! What did you do that for? Right into my eye holes! It's hard enough breathing in here as it goes. Do something useful – help me off with this suit." Wayne began to pull at the ears of his suit. Elmer joined in, wrenching Wayne's head this way and that.

"Hey, hey, hey! That hurts! See how you like it!" Wayne grabbed Elmer's ears and gave them a good waggle. Elmer made a strange whinnying noise and cuffed Wayne round the ear, sending him flying into the bushes. He scampered after him, dragged him out of the bushes by his feet and gave Wayne a huge hug.

"Burggh, urrgh, goodness me! You're stronger than you look. You ought to be careful! Hang on, you've broken the zipper holding on my mask." Wayne peeled off his mask from his red face. "Ah, that's better! What's the matter Elmer? What's up?" Elmer had beads of tears trembling on the lower lids of both eyes and his lower lip quivered. "You sure are acting peculiar, Elmer." Elmer gave a little whimper. "And I tell you what, your outfit is a hell of a lot more realistic than mine, in fact ...." Wayne stopped dead and a strange expression came onto his face. "You're not Elmer are you?" The creature that was not Elmer breathed softly through its nose at him, then slowly, gently leant forward and kissed Wayne on top of his head. It wiped a tear away from its eye with the back of one massive paw. Then on all fours it lolloped into darkness between the bushes.

Wayne stood silently staring into the woods, until an

angry crashing in the undergrowth disturbed him. A hot and angry man in a tattered nylon Sasquatch suit stomped into the clearing.

"There you are! Where were you when those campers were thrashing me with twigs and threatening to set fire to me? That old lady was vicious. Wayne, are you listening to me? Wayne?".

Wayne slowly fell in a faint, first on to his knees and then on to his face.

I wonder what's up with him?" Elmer unzipped the head of his Bigfoot suit and then bent down to help Wayne back onto his feet. "What's the matter Buddy? Seen a real Sasquatch or something? Ha, ha, ha, a real Sasquatch. Sometimes I'm just so funny, I make myself laugh!"

Wayne lifted his face a little out of the large and all too real footprint and groaned.

TIM CRAWLEY

AFTER READING

1 Did you guess what the ending of the story would be? If so, at which point in the story did you begin to sense the likely ending?

2 How do you explain the title?

COMPARE

Discussion

1 Tim Crawley wrote his story for this book after reading the Sasquatch reports. Which details or facts from them has he incorporated into his story?

2 In the second extract, the Sasquatch is presented much more sympathetically than in the first extract. How is this achieved?

Assignments

1 Rewrite Tim Crawley's story from the point of view of the real Bigfoot. How would he describe the human beings he encounters? Would he feel confused, aggressive, nervous? Why is he sad at the end?

2 Look again at the experience of Wayne and Elmer. Write a factual account of their Sasquatch encounter to appear in the Reader's Digest. Look back at the style, content and length of those reports and try to imitate them.

3 Produce a newspaper report describing the events of 'Put Your Best Bigfoot Forward'. To be realistic your report should contain the following:
- headline (attention-grabbing, perhaps involving word play, no more than seven words long)
- topic sentence (the first sentence of a newspaper report always gives the whole story; the rest of the report adds details)
- short paragraphs (one or two sentences long only)
- subheadings to break up paragraphs
- an overall length of around 150 words

Your report should answer these questions: who? what? where? when? why?

EXTRA-TERRESTRIAL ENCOUNTERS

BEFORE READING

Give yourself two minutes to do an initial skim of the article, trying to find the answers to these questions:

1 In the first section, which two countries are referred to as places of UFO sightings?

2 What, in broad outline, was the main event in the Tunguska incident?

3 What is the Sirius mystery?

Compare your answers with those of a friend. Now go back and read the article in greater depth.

■ Sightings of Unidentified Flying Objects are not new. In this section compare the extract from a reference book with a UFO encounter reported in an American newspaper.

READING SKILLS

Reading for meaning

Skimming/scanning

THE INHABITED UNIVERSE?

President Jimmy Carter has seen a flying saucer. It happened in 1973 after he had made a late-evening speech to a Lions Club meeting in Thomaston, Georgia. As he left with a group of friends he saw the UFO, apparently hovering above a field.

"It was a very peculiar aberration, but about 20 people saw it," he told the *National Enquirer* newspaper during his presidential election campaign. "It was the darndest thing I've ever seen. It was big, it was very bright, it changed colours and it was about the size of the Moon. We watched it for 10 minutes, but none of us could figure out what it was. One thing's for sure, I'll never make fun of people who say they've seen unidentified flying objects in the sky!" Carter's 23-year-old son gave the newspaper further details about the UFO: "It had three lights – clustered together about the size of the Moon.

My dad said they were changing colour from red to green. It was positioned off to one side of the Moon."
It is now up to the American President, who is on record as saying "I am convinced UFOs exist because I have seen one," to take time from the burdens of his office and open the UFO files to public inspection – for millions of his countrymen believe that the American authorities know more about UFOs than they are saying.

Many other authorities adopt a secretive policy on UFOs, as can be seen from a statement made in July 1976 by another eminent UFO eye-witness, General Carlos Cavero, commanding officer of the Spanish Air Force in the Canary Islands. While spending a few days near Sabada, a village in a remote part of eastern Spain, he saw a bright UFO travelling at a speed of 22,000 miles per hour. He calculated the speed from the time it took the UFO to travel the 12 miles to the next village – just two seconds. General Cavero said, after reporting his sighting to the Spanish Air Ministry in Madrid: "As an Air Force officer I hold, officially, the same opinions as the Air Ministry. But personally I think these unidentified flying objects come from other planets."

The UFO seen by one of Spain's top serving officers, was also apparently seen by a well-known local doctor, Francisco Padron, who had a close encounter with the object. "It was nearly dark," he said, "and I was driving along a lonely road. Then I saw a round sphere about 40 feet in diameter hovering above the road ahead of me. It was emitting a blueish light and was about 20 feet above the ground. As I approached, my radio cut out but my headlights kept working. I passed right underneath and saw, silhouetted inside through a type of porthole, two very tall figures dressed in bright red. Then it took off and vanished in the direction of Tenerife."

So, despite the official denials and the negative findings of investigations such as the Condon Committee, the flying saucer mystery deepens with an American president and a Spanish air force general among the eye-witnesses in the 1970s. The UFOs refuse to go away; so, again, what are they?

The Tunguska Incident

A giant ball of fire shot across Western China and Mongolia on the morning of June 30, 1908, and exploded with a deafening roar in the desolate marsh region of Tunguska in the heart of Siberia, 2200 miles east of Moscow. Seismographs as far away as Washington registered the event and a series of thunderclaps were heard 500 miles away. A "black rain" of debris fell over a wide area and trees were flattened over an area of 1500 square miles (whereas the Hiroshima atom bomb flattened only 18 square miles). It seemed to be a spectacular meteorite. But there is a mystery: A meteorite that could cause such devastation should have left a gigantic crater on impact, but no crater nor remains of the meteorite have been found. Because of Russia's internal problems, the Siberian explosion was not investigated for 19 years. When Leonid Kulik, a meteorite expert, led an expedition to the area in 1927 he found a charred forest with flattened trees – their roots pointing to the centre of the blast. But strangely, the trees at the centre were still upright. One explanation is that whatever it was that exploded did so high above Tunguska.

In 1976 the Russians announced that a new study of the mystery was to be carried out. This followed the discovery of very strange effects in the area. The Tunguska peat swamps receive their minerals only from the air and they grow at a regular rate, so it has been possible to examine the layer that formed at the time of the great explosion. Silicate particles have been found that are of a composition which not only differs from that found in ordinary meteorites, but has no equivalent in known earthly bodies. Genetic mutations have now been reported from the area and a mighty coniferous forest has blossomed in the once devestated region. The natural rate of genetic change in the region's flora has increased twelvefold, it is said, in which case some exciting discoveries could appear when the Russian expedition publishes its results.

What, then, caused the 1908 Tunguska explosion? It would be easy to dismiss it as just a supermeteorite, or a comet, or even an as-yet-unknown cosmic object that strayed too close to the Earth and exploded in the atmosphere. Some scientists have suggested that it might have been an object made of antimatter that was annihilated by the Earth's matter in a fantastic explosion. Others believe it might have been a small exploding black hole. But there is one disturbing aspect of the Siberian mystery that does not fit any of these theories. From a study of eye-witness accounts of the great ball of fire, Dr Felix Ziegel of the Moscow Institute of Aviation has concluded that the object made a 375-mile arc in the air before crashing or exploding. "That is," says Dr Ziegel, "it carried out a manoeuvre." This has led some scientists to suggest that the Tunguska object was a spacecraft that got into difficulties and crashed or exploded. Perhaps it was the first probe sent out by beings in another solar system and the information it sent back enabled them to build new spaceships – the present-day UFOs – that were able to carry out surveillance of our planet without difficulty.

COLIN WILSON & CHRISTOPHER EVANS
THE GIANT BOOK OF THE UNKNOWN

Dozens witness UFO landing –
now scientists ponder craft's mysterious rings

STARSHIP LANDS IN WHEAT FIELD

As dozens of wide-eyed witnesses stood frozen in their tracks, a gleaming silver space-ship swooped to Earth outside a remote farming community – and two tiny aliens strolled from the craft to look around!

Moments later the jaunty ET-like creatures returned to their ship and zoomed toward the stars, leaving five eerie rings in a wheat field as the only reminder of their visit.

"It was a sight more fantastic than anything in any movie," said stunned farmer Stan Smith.

"I know some people are going to think I'm nuts, but I saw what I saw. I saw a flying saucer come out of the sky – and I saw some little men get off. A lot of other people saw it, too."

AFTER READING

1 Why is the fact that Jimmy Carter apparently saw a UFO significant?

2 Why is a sighting by the Spanish air force general important?

3 What did the 1976 Russian study reveal?

■ This article comes from the *Weekly World News*. The newspaper is published in Florida, USA, but the article is about an incident in Wiltshire, England.

The Earl of Clancarty, head of the UFO Study Group in the British Parliament, didn't see the spaceship, but he did examine the bizarre circles it left behind – and he's convinced Smith and the other witnesses are telling the truth.

"The marks are fascinating, suggesting something has landed there," said the sombre nobleman. The astonishing episode began as hardworking farmhands were taking to the fields in a rural region of Wiltshire, England.

"Suddenly we heard a low droning sound, and when we looked up this big shiny egg-shaped object was hovering there, high above the field," recalled a young woman.

"Everybody stood still and stared. Four or five seconds later the thing swept down into the field about 150 yards away and my heart started pounding.

"The next thing I knew these two – I hate to say it – these two little men were scurrying around near the ship. It was daylight but they were so far away we didn't actually see them pop from the UFO – but they couldn't have come from anywhere else.

"While everyone was straining to see them more clearly, they suddenly popped back into the spaceship and it rose up and out of sight. The whole thing only took a minute or two but it was no hallucination. It was as real as you and I."

Witnesses described these aliens as squatty little creatures no more than 3 feet tall, with stubby arms and legs.

"We all wanted to see their faces, but they were too far away for any kind of look," Smith said. "Anybody who tells you he knows what they looked like in the face is lying."

As their shock wore off, several of the witnesses crept over to the landing site. There in the wheat was a large circular hole, surrounded by four smaller circles – the only souvenirs left by their amazing visitors from space.

But the next day, workers found exactly the same pattern of circles in a barley field in nearby Hampshire.

"Whoever they were – whoever they are – they've sure been busy little guys," said one farmer.

"We just wonder when they are coming back here."

JOE BERGER

AFTER READING

1 What are the main facts of the article?

2 Do you believe what happened here? In pairs briefly discuss why you do or do not believe it.

COMPARE

Discussion

1   With a partner, discuss and note down any new information you have learnt about UFOs from these extracts.

2   In groups, make a list of arguments for and against the existence of UFOs. Have your beliefs changed at all in the light of your reading?

3   Individually, compare the written style of the newspaper article with that of the reference book, looking in particular at:

- vocabulary
- sentence lengths
- probable readership

Then discuss with your group the differences you have noticed.

Assignments

1   Based on what you have read in this unit, and on your previous knowledge, write a 150-word encyclopaedia entry about UFOs, summing up some of the sightings and theories. Write in an impersonal, factual style.

2   Imagine you have just read the *Weekly World News* article and you don't believe a word. Write a 100-word letter to the newspaper expressing your views. Give precise examples of what you think is wrong with the report.

3   Organise a studio discussion to debate the issues of life on other planets. Before you begin, divide up the class to research UFO sightings so you can come up with arguments for and against the issues. One of you should play a UFO expert while another could play a disbelieving scientist.

HAUNTINGS

■ Everyone loves a good ghost story. Here are two of the briefest ever written, followed by a classic nineteenth-century ghost story.

READING SKILLS

Personal response

Analysis of genre

AFTER READING

1 Sum up the storyline in one sentence.

The Look of Death

A young Persian gardener said to his Prince:

'Save me! I met Death in the garden this morning, and he gave me a threatening look. I wish that tonight, by some miracle, I might be far away, in Ispahan.'

The Prince lent him his swiftest horse.

That afternoon, as he was walking in the garden, the Prince came face to face with Death. 'Why,' he asked, 'did you give my gardener a threatening look this morning?'

'It was not a threatening look.' replied Death. 'It was an expression of surprise. For I saw him here this morning, and I knew that I would take him in Ispahan tonight.

JEAN COCTEAU

AFTER READING

1 Sum up the storyline in one sentence.

2 How unexpected was the ending?

■ This story shows Edgar Allan Poe's skill at creating horror.

Ending for a Ghost Story

'How eerie!' said the girl, advancing cautiously. 'And what a heavy door!' She touched it as she spoke and it suddenly swung to with a click.

'Good Lord!' said the man, 'I don't believe there's a handle inside. Why, you've locked us both in!'

'Not both of us. Only one of us', said the girl, and before his eyes she passed straight through the door, and vanished.

I A IRELAND

The Tell-Tale Heart

TRUE! – nervous – very, very dreadfully nervous I had been and am; but why will you say that I am mad? The disease had sharpened my senses – not destroyed – not dulled them. Above all was the sense of hearing acute. I heard all things in the heaven and in the earth. I heard many things in hell. How, then, am I mad? Hearken! and observe how healthily – how calmly I can tell you the whole story.

It is impossible to say how first the idea entered my brain; but once conceived, it haunted me day and night. Object there was none. Passion there was none. I loved the old man. He had never wronged me. He had never given me insult. For his gold I had no desire. I think it was his eye! yes, it was this! He had the eye of a vulture – a pale blue eye, with a film over it. Whenever it fell upon me, my blood ran cold; and so by degrees – very gradually – I made up my mind to take the life of the old man, and thus rid myself of the eye forever.

Now this is the point. You fancy me mad. Madmen know nothing. But you should have seen me. You should have seen how wisely I proceeded – with what caution – with what foresight – with what dissimulation I went to work! I was never kinder to the old man than during the whole week before I killed him. And every night, about midnight, I turned the latch of his door and opened it – oh so gently! And then, when I had made an opening sufficient for my head, I put in a dark lantern, all closed, closed, so that no light shone out, and then I thrust in my head. Oh, you would have laughed to see how cunningly I thrust it in! I moved it slowly, very, very slowly, so that I might not disturb the old man's sleep. It took me an hour to place my whole head within the opening so far that I could see him as he lay upon his bed. Ha! – would a madman have been so wise as this? And then, when my head was well in the room, I undid the lantern cautiously – oh, so cautiously – cautiously (for the hinges creaked) – I undid it just so much that a single thin ray fell upon the vulture eye. And this I did for seven long nights – every night just at midnight – but I found the eye always closed; and so it was impossible to do the work; for it was not the old man who vexed me, but his Evil Eye. And every morning, when the day broke, I went boldly into the chamber, and spoke courageously to him, calling him by name in a hearty tone, and inquiring how he had passed the night. So you see he would have been a very profound old man, indeed, to suspect that every night, just at twelve, I looked in upon him while he slept.

Upon the eighth night I was more than usually cautious in opening the door. A watch's minute hand moves more quickly than did mine. Never before that night, had I *felt* the extent of my own powers – of my sagacity. I could scarcely contain my feelings of triumph. To think that there I was, opening the door, little by little, and he not even to dream of my secret deeds or thoughts. I fairly chuckled at the idea; and perhaps he heard me; for he moved on the bed suddenly, as if startled. Now you may think that I drew back – but no. His room was as black as pitch with the thick darkness (for the shutters were close fastened, through fear of robbers) and so I knew that he could not see the opening of the door, and I kept pushing it on steadily, steadily.

I had my head in, and was about to open the lantern, when my thumb slipped upon the tin fastening, and the old man sprang up in bed, crying out – 'Who's there?'

I kept quite still and said nothing. For a whole hour I did not move a muscle, and in the meantime I did not hear him lie down. He was still sitting up in the bed listening; – just as I have done, night after night, harkening to the death watches in the wall.

Presently I heard a slight groan, and I knew it was the groan of mortal terror. It was not a groan of pain or of grief – oh, no! – it was the low stifled sound that arises from the bottom of the soul when overcharged with awe. I knew the sound well. Many a night, just at midnight, when all the world slept, it has welled up from my own bosom, deepening, with its dreadful terrors that distracted me. I say I knew it well. I knew what the old man felt, and pitied him, although I chuckled at heart. I knew that he had been lying awake ever since the first slight noise, when he had turned in the bed. His fears had been ever since growing upon him. He had been trying to fancy them causeless, but could not.

He had been saying to himself – 'It is nothing but the wind in the chimney – it is only a mouse crossing the floor,' or 'it is merely a cricket which had made a single chirp'. Yes, he had been trying to comfort himself with these suppositions: but he had found all in vain. *All in vain*; because Death, in approaching him, had stalked with his black shadow before him, and enveloped the victim. And it was the mournful influence of the unperceived shadow that caused him to feel – although he neither saw nor heard – to *feel* the presence of my head within the room.

When I had waited a long time, very patiently, without hearing him lie down, I resolved to open a little – a very, very little crevice in the lantern. So I opened it – you cannot imagine how stealthily – until, at length a simple dim ray, like the thread of the spider, shot from out the crevice and fell full upon the vulture eye

It was open – wide, wide open – and I grew furious as I gazed upon it. I saw it with perfect distinctness – all a dull blue, with a hideous veil over it that chilled the very marrow in my bones; but I could see nothing else of the old man's face or person: for I had directed the ray as if by instinct, precisely upon the damned spot.

And have I not told you that what you mistake for madness is but over-acuteness of the senses? – now, I say, there came to my ears a low, dull, quick sound, such as a watch makes when enveloped in cotton. I knew *that* sound well, too. It was the beating of the old man's heart. It increased my fury, as the beating of a drum stimulates the soldier into courage.

But even yet I refrained and kept still. I scarcely breathed. I held the lantern motionless. I tried how steadily I could maintain the ray upon the eye. Meantime the hellish tattoo of the heart increased. It grew quicker and quicker, and louder and louder every instant. The old man's terror *must* have been extreme! It grew louder, I say, louder every moment! – do you mark me well? I have told you that I am nervous: so I am. And now at the dead hour of the night, amid the dreadful silence of that old house, so strange a noise as this excited me to uncontrollable terror. Yet, for some minutes longer I refrained and stood still. But the beating grew louder, louder! I thought the heart must burst. And now a new anxiety seized me – the sound would be heard by a neighbour! The old man's hour had come! With a loud yell, I threw open the lantern and leaped into the room. He shrieked once – once only. In an instant I dragged him to the floor, and pulled the heavy bed over him. I then smiled gaily, to find the deed so far done. But, for minutes, the heart beat on with a muffled sound. This, however, did not vex me; it would not be heard through the wall. At length it ceased. The old man was dead. I removed the bed and examined the corpse. Yes, he was stone, stone dead. I placed my hand upon the heart and held it there many minutes. There was no pulsation. He was stone dead. His eye would trouble me no more.

If still you think me mad, you will think so no longer when I describe the wide precautions I took for the concealment of the body. The night waned, and I worked hastily, but in silence. First of all I dismembered the corpse. I cut off the head and the arms and the legs.

I then took up three planks from the flooring of the chamber, and deposited all between the scantlings. I then replaced the boards so cleverly, so cunningly, that no human eye – not even his – could have detected anything wrong. There was nothing to wash out – no stain of any kind – no blood-spot whatever. I had been too wary for that. A tub had caught all – ha! ha!

When I had made an end of these labours, it was four o'clock – still dark as midnight. As the bell sounded the hour, there came a knocking at the street door. I went down to open it with a light heart, – for what had I *now* to fear? There entered three men, who introduced themselves, with perfect suavity, as officers of the police. A shriek had been heard by a neighbour during the night; suspicion of foul play had been aroused; information had been lodged at the police office, and they (the officers) had been deputed to search the premises.

I smiled, for *what* had I to fear? I bade the gentlemen welcome. The shriek, I said, was my own in a dream. The old man, I mentioned, was absent in the country. I took my visitors all over the house. I bade them search – search well. I led them, at length, to *his* chamber. I showed them his treasures, secure, undisturbed. In the enthusiasm of my confidence, I brought chairs into the room, and desired them here to rest from their fatigues, while I myself, in the wild audacity of my perfect triumph, placed my own seat upon the very spot beneath which reposed the corpse of the victim.

The officers were satisfied. My *manner* had convinced them. I was singularly at ease. They sat, and while I answered cheerily, they chatted of familiar things. But, ere long, I felt myself getting pale and wished them gone. My head ached, and I fancied a ringing in my ears: but still they sat and still chatted. The ringing became more distinct: – it continued and became more distinct: I talked more freely to get rid of the feeling: but it continued and gained definiteness – until, at length, I found that the noise was *not* within my ears.

No doubt I now grew *very* pale; – but I talked more fluently and with a heightened voice. Yet the sound increased – and what could I do? It was *a low, dull, quick sound – much such a sound as a watch makes when enveloped in cotton*. I gasped for breath – and yet the officers heard it not. I talked more quickly – more vehemently; but the noise steadily increased. Why *would* they not be gone? I paced the floor to and fro with heavy strides, as if excited to fury by the observations of the men – but the noise steadily increased. Oh God! what *could* I do? I foamed – I raved – I swore! I swung the chair upon which I had been sitting, and grated it upon the boards, but the noise arose over all and continually increased. It grew louder – louder – *louder!* And still the men chatted pleasantly, and smiled. Was it possible they heard not? Almighty God! – no, no! They heard! – they suspected! – they *knew!* – they were making a mockery of my horror! – this I thought, and this I think. But anything was better than this agony! Anything was more tolerable than this derision! I could bear those hypocritical smiles no longer! I felt that I must scream or die! and now – again! – hark! louder! louder! louder! *louder!*

'Villains!' I shrieked, 'dissemble no more! I admit the deed! – tear up the planks! here, here! – it is the beating of his hideous heart!'

EDGAR ALLAN POE

AFTER READING

1 Look back at the first paragraph of the story. What are your first impressions of the narrator?

2 The narrator says 'You fancy me mad'. What clues are we given throughout the story that he is mad? What signs are there that he isn't?

COMPARE

Discussion

1   What are the ingredients of a good ghost story? Use this list as a starting-point, adding your own ideas, and placing them in alphabetical order:

- set in the past
- mysterious characters
- old-fashioned language
- suspense
- horror
- ghosts
- plenty of atmosphere
- an eerie setting – eg old house, foggy night, etc
- an unexpected ending

Look back at the three ghost stories in this unit. How well do the different ingredients apply to each of them?

2   'I knew what the old man felt, and pitied him, although I chuckled at heart'. What do you make of the narrator of *The Tell-Tale Heart* from this sentence? What kind of person is he? Discuss your opinions in small groups.

3   Look again at the narrator's murder of the old man. How would the effect on the readers have differed if the description had been more detailed and bloodthirsty?

Assignments

1 Write your own ghost story set in an 'unghostly' setting, such as one of those listed below. Try to scare the reader without using the old techniques of haunted houses, headless people and so on. Make it a modern ghost story.

Some unghostly settings:
- a supermarket
- a kitchen at noon
- a pet shop
- an aircraft in mid-air

2 Write a two-page essay about your reaction to Poe's story. Perhaps it reminds you of other stories that you have read or seen. The story was written around a hundred years ago – what signs are there of this in the content, sentences and vocabulary. What did you find enjoyable or difficult about reading it?

3 Imagine you are the chief of police investigating this murder. Retell events from your point of view, starting with your arrival at the house to interview the suspect. Refer back to Edgar Allan Poe's story and try to keep the order of events exactly the same.

WIDER READING

Unexplained Mysteries
The following books contain factual accounts of subjects such as UFOs, ghosts and other unexplained phenomena:

Colin Wilson and Christopher Evans, *The Giant Book of the Unknown*; Reader's Digest, *Mysteries of the Unexplained*; Brad Steiger, *Mysteries of Time and Space*; Len Ortzon, *Strange Stories of UFOs*.

Ghost Stories
There are dozens of ghost-story collections available. The following are particularly recommended:

Robert Westall, *Ghost Stories* and *Ghosts and Journeys*; Penelope Lively, *Uninvited Ghosts* and *The Man in Black: Macabre Stories from Fear on Four*; Susan Hill, *The Woman in Black* and *The Mist in the Mirror*; Richard Peyton, *The Ghost Now Standing on Platform One*; Robert Phillips, *The Omnibus of 20th-Century Ghost Stories*; M R James, *Selected Ghost Stories*.

AFTER READING

1 Choose three ghost stories which you have enjoyed reading and write a comparison of the main characters in them.

2 Choose one 'mysterious' subject that interests you and write an introduction to the topic for someone unfamiliar with it. Use references to your reading to back up your points.

LIFESTYLES

In the last fifty years there have been greater changes than ever before in the way that people live. Technology enables us to do things that our ancestors did not even dream about; yet in other ways, our lives have not altered greatly from the way people lived hundreds of years ago.
- *Do children want to lead similar lives to those of their parents?*
- *What have we, in our technological age, lost, and what have we gained when we compare our lives with those of people who lived many years ago?*
- *What effect does our lifestyle have upon our health?*

GENERATION GAP

■ A Jamaican father living in London telephones his son with good news.

Edication

Hello operata,
Kin you get me Kingston Jamaica sah?
I wanta speak to mah boy Bobby,
de numba is
JA five zero zero five.
How yah mean wha' JA stan fuh?
Wha' wrong wid yo'
it stan fuh Kingston Jamaica man.

Berr berr, berr berr, br...
Dat you Bobby?
Whasa matta son, you alrite?
Dint I always tell you
I gwine give you ah big surprise?
Well son, yo' lucky day come at las'.
Mek I tell you son,
yo' ole Ma win de London football.....

What?

You mean you neva hear bout de football pools?

Oh,

well is dat I win.

How what?
De line bad man,
ah seh de line bad man!
Can' hear a ting ya seh.
Oh, how much!
Fifty thousand son,
fifty thousand pounds.
Ef I comin' home?
Ya mean to JA?
Wha' do ya boy,
of course I comin' home,
not before I buy you all what you need dough,
ah got you most everyting a'ready,
    from mail orda,
I even bought you a bran' new use' car.
Ah doan tink you preciate what I doin'
    for you Bobby,
doan tink you preciate it at all.

What you tryin' to seh?
Rupert Ma bought 'im what!
Bought 'im edication?
Is you gone crazy Bobby?
You doan have to worry bout Rupert,
yo' Ma got money now,
you jus' fine out where Rupert Ma got it
I will get it if you wants it son,
you doan have to explain anyting.

God, dis young generation got such funny tase,
I neva tase College in mah life;
how you cook it son,
wid rice?
I hear one of de woman at de People Social Club
braggin' bout er chil'ren goin' to Univercity,
Mussa some home in de country.

Hear one of dem:

'My girl Jermin goin' Oxford,
she gwine get good edication dere,
like de rich folks.
Wen she gets her scrolls I gwine put dem
    in frame'.

For dem boastin',
de Holy Saint done scratch dem off him book.
Talk talk talk all de time, bout wat dem chile do.

Wat ya mean I done undastan'?
Oh.....ya seh college is ah school?
Course ah know dat.
But wait!
College really supply all dose tings you seh?
I is a real fool man;
Good ting you got booklearning son,
so w'en we is out in company, yo' ole Ma doan
    shame yo'.

Nex' club nite I gwine mek dem crazy,
specially w'en I tell dem you gwine to college
    too.
What ya say?
You wants to be a lawyer?
Bless yo' sweet little heart.
I gwine give you de bigges' sen-off
London town eva see.
I will get my bank to sen' yo' passage befo' de
    cock crow.
So I see ya w'en I see ya;
But rememba dis w'en ya come,
no blonds, jes' edication.

RUDOLPH KIZERMAN

AFTER READING

1 What is the good news that the father wants to tell his son?

2 Which lines in the poem tell us that the father is disappointed with his son's reaction to his news?

<table>
<tr><td>

Discussion

1   In pairs, discuss what the father thinks 'College' and 'Univercity' mean.

2   What kind of lifestyle does the son want for himself? In what ways is it different from the one that his father planned for him?

</td><td colspan="2">

Assignments

1   In pairs, work out what the son says to his father during the telephone conversation. Then act out a conversation based on the poem. One of you should take the part of the father, and one the part of the son.

2   Write an essay about how you would change your lifestyle if you won fifty thousand pounds. Is there anything that you would definitely not change?

</td></tr>
</table>

DIARY WRITING

■ Samuel Pepys and Anne Hughes wrote their diaries in the seventeenth and eighteenth centuries. Pepys lived from 1633 to 1703. He rose from humble beginnings to become a very successful business man, popular with the nobility of his day. He kept a diary for thirty-six years, in which he recorded every aspect of his life.

READING SKILLS
Summarising
Analysing language

Samuel Pepys's Diary

21 June 1662

Having from my wife and from the maids complaints made of the boy, I called him up and with my whip did whip him till I was not able to stir, and yet I could not make him confess any of the lies that they tax him with. At last, not willing to let him go away a conqueror, I took him in task again and pulled off his frock to his shirt, and whipped him till he did confess that he did drink the Whay, which he hath denied. And pulled a pinke, and above all, did lay the candlesticke upon the ground in his chamber, which he hath denied this Quarter of this year. I confess it is one of the greatest wonders that ever I met with, that such a little boy as he could possibly be able to suffer half so much as he did to maintain a lie. But I think I must be forced to put him away. So to bed, with my arme very weary.

25 June 1662

Up by 4 a-clock and put my accounts with my Lord into a very good order, and so to my office – where having put many things in order, I went to the Wardrobe but find my Lord gone to Hampton Court. After discourse with Mr. Sheply, we parted and I into Thames street beyond the bridge and there enquired among the shops the price of tarr and oyle; and do find great content in it and hope to save the King money by this practice. So home to dinner and then to the Change; and so home again and at the office, preparing business against tomorrow all the afternoon. At night walked with my wife upon the leads; and so to supper and to bed. My [wife] having lately a great paine in her eare, for which this night she begins to take phisique; and I have got cold and so have a great deal of my old pain.

26 June 1662

Up and took phisique, but such as to go abroad with, only to loosen me, for I am bound. So to the office – and there all the morning, setting till noon; and then took Commissioner Pett home with me to dinner, where my stomach was turned when my sturgeon came to table, upon which I saw very many little worms creeping, which I suppose was through the staleness of the pickle. He being gone, comes Mr. Nicholson, my old fellow-student at Magdalen, and we played three or four things upon violin and Basse; and so parted, and I to my office till night; and then came Mr. Sheply and Creede in order to setting some accounts of my Lord right; and so to bed.

29 June 1662

Lords Day. Up by 4 a-clock, and to the settling of my own accounts, and I do find upon my monthly ballance (which I have undertaken to keep from month to month) that I am worth 650 *l*, the greatest sum that ever I was yet master of. I pray God give me a thankful spirit, and care to improve and increase it.

22 November 1668

Lords day. My wife and I lay long, with mighty content, and so rose, and she spent the whole day making herself clean, after four or five weeks being in continued dirt. And I knocking up nails and making little settlements in my house, till noon; and then eat a bit of meat in the kitchen, I all alone, and so to the office to set down my Journall, for some days leaving it imperfect, the matter being mighty grievous to me and my mind from the nature of it. And so in to solace myself with my wife, whom I got to read to me, and so W. Hewer and the boy; and so after supper, to bed. This day, my boy's Livery is come home, the first I ever had of Greene lined with red; and it likes me well enough.

Samuel Pepys

Samuel Pepys

24 December 1668

A cold day. Up and to the office, where all the morning alone at the office, nobody meeting, being the Eve of Christmas. At noon home to dinner and then to the office, busy all the afternoon, and at night home to supper; and it being now very cold, and in hopes of a frost, I begin this night to put on a Wastecoate, it being the first winter in my whole memory that ever I stayed till this day before I did so. So to bed, in mighty good humour with my wife, but sad in one thing, and that is for my poor eyes.

25 December 1668

Christmas day. Up, and continued on my waistcoat, the first day this winter. And I to church, where Ald. Backewell coming in late, I beckoned to his lady to come up to us; who did, with another lady; and after sermon I led her down through the church to her husband and coach – a noble, fine woman, and a good one – and one my wife shall be acquainted with. So home and to dinner alone with my wife, who, poor wretch, sat undressed all day till 10 at night, altering and lacing of a black petticoat – while I by her, making the boy read to me the life of Julius Caesar and Des Cartes book of music – the latter of which I understand not, nor think he did well that writ it, though a most learned man. Then after supper made the boy play upon his lute, which I have not done twice before sence he came to me; and so, my mind in mighty content, we to bed.

31 December 1668

Blessed be God, the year ends, after some late very great sorrow with my wife by my folly; yet ends, I say, with great mutual peace and content – and likely to last so by my care, who am resolved to enjoy the sweet of it which I now possess, by never giving her like cause of trouble. My greatest trouble is now from the backwardness of my accounts, which I have not seen the bottom of now near these two years, so that I know not in what condition I am in the world; but by the grace of God, as fast as my eyes will give me leave, I will do it.

Diary of a farmer's wife

Anne Hughes kept a diary from 1769-97. Her life was centred on the farm and on her household. She wrote in secret, often when her husband was asleep in bed.

Today hav John and I bin wed this 3 yere and here I do set down all that I do every day.

Today I did do my butter maken, leving Sarah to cook most of the dinner, as the butter was longe time cummin, indeed not till John had put in a crown piece and turned did it cum. Sarah did burne the dinner, like she always do, and John was very cross therebye, he mislyking Sarahs cooken, so I do sometimes hav to let him think it is me. Men be verry tiresome sometimes.

FEB. YE 8 – This morn John in with the newes that Parson Willum Ellis will preche at our church cum Sunday, and will ette with us, for which I be sorrie for he do ette so much mete, it do give me much work cooken. John likes to hav a good table when folkes do cum, so carters wiffe and Sarah will have to help me. I shall wear my purple silk cum Sunday. John bein the biggest farm-holder here-about I do hav to keep up with it, but it does wearie my whiles.

FEB. YE 10. – Parson and Mistress Ellis come earlie and did ett a good meal of bread and cheese, and did drink 2 juggs of cyder. Then we to church after me tellen Sarah what to doe, and where to putt the dishes on the tabel. Mistress Ellis comin I did fetch out all my silver and glass so to make a shine, she haven littel to her name as I do know. There was much mudd to walk in to church. John not haven a cart out on the Sabbeth day, we futts it. She minsed along aside me prating of her new cloathes and that the gown she is waring cost so much, which I doe know is onlie her last yeres turned about and new bowes on for show. This I cappes by saying I will show her my new brockade which John brought me last market day, he havin got the better of old Skinnie-flinte Tom over some hay he did sell him. She be verrie jellous, not ansuring when I do tell her of the new gown. The sermon very dry, with some hard nockes at the folks which he do not like. John did nod and I did praye that Sarah would not brake the dishes, or ett any of the little things which she doe some wiles, when my back be turned. Sermon lasted 2 houres, then we out and home to dinner. I did see Farmer Wells and his mistress looking prosperous, he no doubt have sold his straw, so a few ginneas to spend. Verrie glad was I to see Sarah had done all verrie well, the tabel lookinge good; and I did see Mistress Ellis was imprested by my glass and silver forkes and spoones, albeit she nott wanting to show it but woode have us think hers was as good, which I do doubt.

A great lot etten, she having 3 bigg slivers off the mutten, and pestering me the wye and warefore off the new taste, which I do turn off by saying the wether be well for the time of the yer; until I could see she was wroth trying not to show it outards, saying that she would ett no more; bein afraid the flavour would disagree with her, which I doute not, she ettin so much.

After we had dined, I did take her to my sleepin chamber to show off on her my best cloes; at seein which, she begins to trump up about her new black sylk which had cost so much, and which I do know she did buy of Mary Ann herself telling me so. Knowing this I could well afford to bring out my black sylk with the white spottes, what John did buy for me an which I had not put on. This did end her bounce so down again, it being two howers since she had fed, to tee drinken.

She did offer to help, butt I tell her Sarah do know what to do, me knowing well that Madam did only want to see my larder shelfs, she bein a nosie person.

So into the parlur, where Sarah busie; mee hitchen to help, but did not, bein a ladye for the day.

After tee drinking, did start to hint it would soon be dark. And she did fish for a night visit, which I made not to hear; and did pack her up a bag of eggs and butter as a hint to be gone. Which they both did, to our content; we bein tired to their caddel. He a little peart with Johns wine did go home tittering; but she verrie prim and proper. We in to the kitchen where I did ketch Sarah ettin a slice of ham; which I forgave her as she had praised me in front of Mistress Ellis, which pleased me. John cummin in to see what vittles was left, he did lock it up. So we to bed, me bein tired.

FEB. YE 14. – This be Saint Val's day and this morn I did see Sarah cum in from the milking looking all red about the cheek and her cap awry. I bein curious did stop her, and she did say Carter Trues son did say he was her

Valentine, and she had said yes. She did giggel a great deal and I did tell her to get on with her work, and not to be a silly wench; but I fear me there will be much whisperings and kissen going on, they bein both young.

I must be watchful of Sarah and see she do not neglect the calfs and pigges and hens, which do now lay good egges; which is good for me, as John do let me keep hen monies for my pokett, which do suit me much.

JUNE YE 22. – Laste night after me abed, I did heare a step outeside, and I to the winder; where I did see Sarah off to the stabel yarde. It being 12 of the clocke, I did dress and follow to see whats adoe to the stabel; where she did stop, and me standing by the straw stacke did hear her say: Hempseed I sowe, and he thats my true love cum to me nowe. Then I did see what the sillie wench were doing; she sowing the seed where the carters lad do walk, and his big feet crumping it, the smell there of would reach his nose and so make him to turn to her from all the other wenches. Me knoeing the sillie wench was safe, back to bed; when I did hear her creep in later.

This set me thinking of how I did do the same thing before I did marrie John, me bein sillie likewise. The next day he did ask me to wed, but I did find out later that he did not goe neare where I did strew the hempen seede. So I doute me if Sarahs charme will worke.

AUG. YE 23. – Me and Sarah bein bussie with lime washen of the kitchen and house place, John hav to feed the pigges and calfs, which do fuss him much; and the big boar pigg biting him hard on the leg, he cums in most wrotheful, and sayes he will hav us out cum tomorrow. At which I do say how can we when we so bussie? So he off out agen after hitting the cat with my pewter pepper pot.

Then in cums Sarah with her hand all bloddie, and she crieing, saying she did do it with the big carver. This I do wash and tye with a peece of old shirt.

John in agen do say whats ado, and me telling him, he mighty cross, saying it be all done apurpus to vex him and to go out to help him. Indeed he be verrie wroth.

At this I be so cross I uppes and sayes Sarah be my maid not his, and he to get out of my kitchen till his temper be better. So he out, shutting the door with a grate noise, saying that wimmen was the verrie divvell; at which I so wrothe I did throw a lump of bredd at him, but only hit the shut doore. Then I did pictur to myself Johns face if I had hit him, and fell to laffing so hartilie that the tears did run adown my cheekes. John do think he be such a grett man, but lord he be just a bigge sillie.

Then me telling Sarah all, she do say: make him a pan cake, and he soone better. So she off to bring sum egges warm from the neste, and we set to makeing agen John do cum in. I did also get a bottle of my fuzzy wine, this being a grate favourit of his.

Now Sarah who be a sensie maid do say, here he cums; and do start to say how happie she be to be living with us and what a good master John is, and her plase here so much better and higher up than anie other farmers plase anie ware, and he as good looking gentleman as anie here.

I do look at John from my eye corner and sense he lookes verrie pleased, not knowing it be all apurpus. Then he inside to say give him the paile for to fetch in the egges, which Sarah does.

Later we to supper, and John etting his bellie full do say the fuzzy wine be grand, and to give Sarah a tott, she being a good wench and respectful to her betters. This I do, and Sarah did thank him verrie prettie, and wishing him good luck did drunke it uppe.

SEPT. YE 5. – We up earlie yester morn and Carters wiffe her by 5 off the clocke. She to the washeing. John and Sarah to the yardes, the while I do cook the breakfast agen they be reddie; with a gret platter full for Carters wiffe in the back house. John sayeing fat lambes be making a good price, he off with sum to markett; and me to the butter makeing. After a bussie morn, we reddie for our meale betimes, carters wiffe setting me and Sarah, much to her delight, she sayeing that when she do go to Farmer Jonses to help with the washeing, they do put her a rabbitts jimmie and naught else but taties and a cup of cider, in the wash hous; and to pay her but 2 pense for her dayes work. Wereby she sayes she will always cum to me first, seeing that her platter be always as good as my own and well payed for what she dows. This be trew, me paying her 4 pense a day and withe oddses to her baskiett.

Sarah bein verrie strange and not speaking, I do think I will ask later what is afute.

Then other divers jobbes, till in cums carters wiffe to say the piggs be fedd and she off agen to the cows milkeing; Sarah to feed the calfs and hens. They in later for their tee, and carters wiffe home with sum oddses for her supper from my cubbord.

Then I do say to Sarah what is the matter with her all day, at which she do start to howl, ande I do say, what is it? And after her howleing a bit she do say carters lad be walking out with Bella Griffin, and did pass he by and not look at her; but that Bella did giggle at her in passeing; and that she do hate carters lad, and do hope he will be off for a soljer out of her way. At this I do tell her to drie her teares, and let him go his gaite, and take no more notice of him. Then Sarah did say he be welcum to Bella, for all she did care. Then, said I, what was she crying for like a pigge? And that I was ashamed of her howleing, their being plentie of lads to go acourteing. At which she sayes she do hate men, and a pittie they be borne at all; wimmen bein so much the kinder; at which I do laff and she dried her teeres, and to work. But I will talk to Carters lad later, not likeing Sarah to be sorried so.

DEC. YE 27. – Christmas be all over now, and our visitors gone, but a right good time we did have, the roads did dry up a bit so not too bad for the travellers, who did cum pack horse. Cusson Tom and Emma, her ladd and his sweetheart Jan, did get here after a journie of hard going Christmas Eve, the rest did cum christmas morning and all of us to church leaving carters wiffe and Sarahs sister Jane to help Sarah with the dinner to be all ready genst our cumming back, and mother and me did set the tables together in a rown and cover them with my linnen table cloths; then we did put the silver and glass and all did look verrie fine. Passon did give a verrie good sermon, tellin us to do to others as we would have them do to us, and the world the better place, to which I do agree. The singing did go right heartilie with a great roar, the church bein full, for all do like the young passon and his mother.

Then we out and home to our dinner. John did set at one end with the beef and geese, and Farmer Ellis at the other to cut up the hams and so on, which Sarah and Jane did carry round till all served, and all did eat their fill and had plentie. Then John did pass the wine and all did drink each other's healths; then the men did smoke while we ladies did drink our wine and talk of divers things that had happened through the year, not thinking so much had; then the men did say let us dance, so Bill and Jen did play a merrie jig on their fiddles and we did step it out finely; till all breathless, we do sit down laffing much.

Farmer Bliss did say lets have a story, so Passon did tell us a good one that did cause much merriment; then John did say he would tell them the story what happened when his father died, and did tell of the man what stopped him on the road. His mother did say it must have bin Joe Graves who did go to them for shelter when in trouble, and they did hide him for 3 days and he getting off safe at last. Then said Mistress Prue it showed how one good turn did make another.

Then cusson Tom saying we be getting too serious, so Mistress Prue to the spinette to play a merrie tune, and we to dancing once more stepping it right merrilie till Sarah do say its time for tea; whereon we do sit down and do justice to all the good things provided, which did make a brave show and looked verrie good on the dishes; the lights from the tapers in Johns mothers silver candle sticks did light the holly Sarah had put on the table in glasses. All the ladies did like mothers meat cake, and want to know how to make it.

Then we did gather together and play the game of Popp; we did put the chairs in a ringe, the men on one side, the ladies on the other with our hands behind, one holding a apple which be passed from one to another. The man must not speak but do beckon to the lady they think have got the apple; if she have not she do say 'popp' and the man do have to sit on the floor and pay forfitt, till all there; but if he be right he do take the ladie on his knees till the game be played out. After we did play bobbie apple, and snap dragon, the Passon burning his fingers mitilie to get Sarahs plum; all did enjoy it much, and then we did stop a while for sum cakes and wine, and sum songs by one and other; then more dancing till supper, then more games and later all home after a really good Christmas which we did all enjoy much with everybody happie. And now this be the last page in my little book. I know not if I shall ever write another one. I do feel I have much to be thankful for, my life with John and his mother be a verrie happy one.

I do wonder where my little book will go, who may read it. I shall always keep it, and perhaps if God do give me a son he will read it some day and so know what a fine man his father is. So I say good-by to my little book.

AFTER READING

1 Do you think that Anne is happy with her life? What about Sarah?

2 How would you describe Anne Hughes to someone who had not read her diary?

COMPARE

Discussion

1   In pairs, devise a chart showing a typical day that Samuel Pepys might have spent, and a typical day that Anne Hughes might have spent. Begin the chart when Samuel and Anne get up in the morning, and end it with their going to bed. From your chart discuss and list five differences in the way that Samuel Pepys and Anne Hughes lived their lives.

2   What have you learned about the lives of servants from reading the diaries?

3   Working in pairs, look carefully at the beginning of the diary entry that Anne Hughes made for 23 August. Read from the first line beginning "Me and Sarah bein bussie..." to the end of the first section. "Indeed he be verrie wrothe." Translate the following phrases into modern English:

- Me and Sarah bein bussie
- John hav to feed the pigges and calfs, which do fuss him much
- he cums in most wrotheful
- So he off out agen
- John in agen do say whats ado
- Indeed he be verrie wroth

Reread Samuel Pepys's diary and make a list of the words whose spellings have changed. Which of the diary extracts was easier to read and why? Even though Pepys's diary is older, his English is more like ours. Why? Would it be better if we could spell words as we liked or is it simpler to have standard spellings as we do now?

Assignments

1   What do you learn from reading the two diaries about the following aspects of people's lives in the seventeenth and eighteenth centuries in the town and country? Make notes under the following headings:

- entertainment
- food
- customs

2   Using the title 'That was then, this is now' and the notes that you have made, write an essay about the way in which certain aspects of life have changed while others have remained the same since Samuel Pepys and Anne Hughes wrote their diaries. Conclude your essay by stating in which time you would prefer to live and why.

3   Write your own diary for a week. Remember that it is the familiar happenings that people find most interesting – the people that you meet, daily events, your feelings at particular moments.

YOUNG PEOPLE NOWADAYS

■ The following newspaper article and play extract examine the age of extremes in which today's teenagers live. We know what is happening across the world, but we may not know the people who live down the street. We worry about the environment, yet we devour the earth's resources more quickly than in any other age. We are better fed and have better health care than any other generation, yet today's teenagers may be more unhealthy than their parents were.

READING SKILLS

Reading for meaning

Identifying key points

Seeking information

MORE FAT THAN FIT

HAS A COUCH POTATO MENTALITY TAKEN HOLD OF BRITAIN'S YOUNG?
STEVE CONNOR INVESTIGATES

A sensual and temperate youth delivers a worn-out body to old age – CICERO

SENTIMENTS that depict today's youth as slothful ne'er-do-wells, weak and feeble compared with past generations, are as old as history.

The latest example comes from Peterborough, where last week the city council reported that school children risk ill-health through inactivity; they are watching videos and playing computer games rather than running or playing football in the park.

Parents have come under a barrage of advice, which takes it as read that their children's health is at increasing risk from modern living. They are urged to encourage children to exercise more and eat a balanced diet, avoiding junkfood and sugar. They are told that their children's ears and eyes are at risk from headphones and screens, that a diet of violent videos and computer games will addle their brains, that letting them wear trainers all day will make their feet soft, sweaty and liable to athlete's foot. (The Royal Marines complain that teenage recruits have never been in worse shape, their feet so soft they cannot go on long marches and their upper body muscles weak from under-use.)

Greater post-war affluency has not led to better bodies, say critics of today's young. At school, pupils can lunch on pizza, chips and chocolate. Many schools no longer enforce hours of outdoor games. Above all, there is television and the computer. A survey of two schools by Peterborough council's leisure department found middle-class children, able to afford the latest gadgets, worse affected than working-class children, who are more likely to run around outdoors in their spare time.

Although the study looked at physical agility rather than health, Chris Blackshaw, the council's assistant sports development officer, said the findings appeared to support the general view that the youth of today were not as fit as they should be. "The general health and fitness of children across the board has deteriorated in recent years", he said.

But Dr Stuart Logan, senior lecturer at the Institute of Child

Health in London, said it was not his experience that working-class children were more active, at least in inner London where there was a dearth of places to play. "I suspect there is some truth in the feeling that in general the children of today are less active," he said. "However, there is no question that the general health of children has improved beyond recognition in recent history, even in the last 15 years."

Dr Tom Sanders, a nutritionist at King's College, London, is emphatic that much of the improvement is due to a better diet, particularly in the first two years of childhood, which can largely determine general health in later life. "Nutritional status has improved immeasurably in the past 50 years," he said. Intake of vitamin C, for instance, had more than doubled since the 1960s. Deaths from heart disease in young men in the past few years had fallen by more than a third, largely because of the switch away from saturated animal fats.

The health problems of today's youth, he said, were often due to an increased opportunity to eat, leading to obesity (which has increased in women by about 12 per cent in the last 10 years) or to eating disorders such as anorexia or bulimia.

There had also been a very big increase in the opportunity to sit for hours and be entertained, whether by television, videos, computer games or personal stereos. Lack of exercise clearly worried many parents; but so did the thought of letting their youngsters play in streets.

What little research there has been into children's viewing habits had not shown any detrimental effect on intellectual development. A study by David Regis at the schools health education unit at Exeter University found that children who watched most television were also most likely to read a book for pleasure.

"We do have some evidence that youngsters who watch a lot of television are less at ease meeting members of the opposite sex, but it's complex," Dr Sanders said. And long hours in front of a TV computer screen lead to a sedentary culture.

Neil Armstrong, reader in exercise science at Exeter University, has undertaken detailed research into childhood activity, monitoring the heart rate of schoolchildren to see what level of exercise they take during a typical day.

He found that more than half the girls, and more than a third of the boys, did not experience the equivalent of a 10-minute brisk walk. He also found that, as girls got older, they progressively became less active and suggested this was due to them taking after their inactive mothers.

It seems the youth of today have never had a better start to life, and many of the genuine problems – such as loss of

1 Do you recognize any aspects of your life in this report?

2 Do you disagree with the criticisms that the writer makes of the way that young people live their lives?

■ Sue is a member of a women's athletic team called the Golden Girls. She is being trained by her father, Noël. Laces is the team's trainer.

hearing clarity due to listening to personal stereos, or athlete's foot from wearing sweaty trainers – are largely self-inflicted.

Even the average height of children is increasing, although there are still significant differences in social class, according to Dr Logan.

Margaret Thatcher was perhaps being prophetic when she said in 1975 on a tour of the United States: "Let our children grow tall, and some taller than others if they have it in them to do so."

THE INDEPENDENT

The Golden Girls

ACT ONE, SCENE TWO

Darkness. Out of the darkness the sound of a runner running. Lights up to pre-dawn. The runner is SUE.

SUE. You know which direction you're going in at home. The north slopes and the south. The south slopes have posh houses. The ones that get the sunlight. There's a saying there about downhill being uphill but it's all running on the flat here. No hills. No view out over it all. You could go on and on. The time was when I thought there must be something would me stop before the horizon. A tree, mountain, mole hill. Some obstacle. Nothing. Just further and further to go. On and on towards the sun. *(She continues to run.)*

Enter NOËL with a stopwatch

The floodlights come on. NOËL times the stopwatch to his own watch, counting. Enter LACES.

LACES. Morning.

NOËL *nods. The stopwatch is obviously broken.*

NOËL. Can you lend us a stopwatch? This is broken. Forty-two seconds and then stops dead.

LACES. Give it to the East Germans.

NOËL. Glad somebody can laugh.

LACES. They'd make no bones about it being a record attempt. The psyching was brilliant.

NOËL. Sue knows not to let a thing like that throw her.

LACES. If you're pysched for long enough, well enough, you've got no chance of winning.

NOËL. She knows she's got twenty-one seconds in her legs.

LACES. If she doesn't over do it.

NOËL. I know what her legs can do.

LACES. I think you should watch it. Lay up a bit. Do you think she should be out this morning?

NOËL. Why's today different?

MIKE *runs across the stage.*

LACES, She's run four races in two days.

NOËL. Sue knows how much effort you have to put in before you dare hope for a bit of magic.

LACES. And if there's no magic?

NOËL. You do without.

MIKE. Morning.

LACES. Morning.

NOËL. It's wasting her to use her at less than 200 meters.

LACES. Do you want me to drop her from the squad?

NOËL. You've got us over a barrel. She needs the facilities.

LACES. I'd like it back. (*He gives* NOËL *the stopwatch.*)

NOËL. Ta.

LACES. Tell her not to push it too much. (LACES *jogs off.*)

NOËL. One minute recovery.

SUE. I hate running tired. Running with your mind, not your body. Waiting for the moment when the two fuse. Knowing that some days they won't. That all it will have been is putting on your tee-shirt, your tracksuit. Trying your laces. The routine. Other days the most perfect, perfect thing. No thoughts at all. Absolute symmetry in your head. Like the perfect races when you know just what to do. Not yesterday, a ragbag of tactics and strategy. I could feel the clock in my head. Time running out. And knowing every fraction of a second that there wasn't going to be a moment which lasted for ever.

NOËL *shows her the time on the stopwatch.*

NOËL. AGAIN.

SUE. No.

NOËL. I said again.

SUE. No.

NOËL. Don't take that tone with me, miss.

SUE. I can't better that.

NOËL. You can and you will.

Pause.

You're a winner, love. You just have to get it together. Then it won't be living in a camper for decent facilities. You'll have everything you deserve. A pretty girl like you, Sue. Think about it.

SUE. It's impossible.

NOËL. It's not, love. I've shown you it's not. You're a winner, love. From the day you were born.

SUE. Don't throw that at me.

NOËL. You were a winner then.

SUE. Don't tell me that.

NOËL. She'd be proud.

SUE. Not listening.

NOËL. Me proud then. Crack it and you can stay in bed for ever.

SUE. Who wants to stay in bed in a camper?

NOËL. If you want everything they've got here.

Pause.

What do you want?

She shakes her head.

We'll go home. I'll drive you twenty miles there and back everyday. But you still won't get the half of what they've got here.

SUE. I can't run any faster for you, Dad –

NOËL. Then run it for yourself. Come on. Again.

LOUISE PAGE

AFTER READING

1 Laces, the team's trainer, tells Noël that he should "watch it". What is he warning Noël about?

2 Why do you think Noël is so keen for Sue to do well? Discuss this with your partner.

COMPARE

Discussion

1   With your partner, discuss and note down as many words as you can think of to describe the lifestyle of the teenagers described in 'More Fat than Fit', and the lifestyle of Sue in *The Golden Girls*.

2   In small groups, discuss the dangers of doing too little exercise, and the dangers of doing too much.

Assignments

1 Work in groups to stage the scene from *The Golden Girls*. When working on the scene, think about the following points:

- What can you learn from the scene about the relationship between the different characters? How can you show this in the way they deliver their lines, the way they stand, the way they look at each other?

- How are you going to stage the scene? Where will your characters stand? How will they move?

2 Write another scene in the play. Your scene could be based on the following ideas:

- Sue talks to Laces about the pressure that she is put under by her father. Laces gives her some advice.

- Sue tells her father that she wants to give up racing.

3 In what ways is it argued in 'More Fat than Fit' that young people are becoming more unhealthy? The following headings might be useful:

Exercise   Food   Entertainment

Then list the ways in which the experts think that young people are becoming healthier. Find out as much information as possible about the way to lead a healthy lifestyle. Your doctor's surgery is a good place to find leaflets on eating well and keeping fit. Your local library and your school library should also have books containing useful information.

4 Using the title, 'More Fat than Fit' and the information that you have collected as a result of your research, write a ten-point guide for teenagers aimed at giving them clear advice about how to lead a healthy lifestyle. Your guide should alert young people to the dangers of being unhealthy as well as giving them advice about how to improve their lifestyles. Think carefully about how you will set out your guide so that the information in it is easy to read and to understand. Think also about the illustrations that you will use to reinforce the points that you want to make.

WIDER READING

Diaries

For a diary with a more contemporary feel, see: *The Secret Diary of Adrian Mole* by Sue Townsend. *The Diary of Anne Frank* was written while Anne was in hiding from the Nazis, and is a testimony to hope and humanity under the most frightening and stressful conditions. Other recommended diaries are *Dorothy Wordsworth's journals*, and *The Penguin Book of Diaries*, edited by Ronald Blythe.

Lifestyles

Among books that examine different lifestyles, the following are recommended: *Why the Whales Came* by Michael Morpurgo, *The Kitchen God's Wife* by Amy Tan, *Sumitra's Story* by Rushkana Smith. Two pioneering women travellers tell their stories in *A Winter in Arabia* by Freya Stark and *Teaching A Stone To Talk* by Annie Dillard.

AFTER READING

1 Read a diary from a time or a culture different from your own, and write an essay saying what you have learnt while reading it.

2 Compare two characters that you have read about in two works of fiction, and describe the similarities and differences in their lifestyles.

CRIME FILE

Our society seems obsessed by crime. Some people say that we glorify it. Crime dominates television, both in drama and documentary programmes and creates the storylines for many of the films we watch.

- *Why do you think people are so fascinated by crime?*
- *Why are crime thrillers so popular for reading and watching?*
- *Is our society becoming more unlawful?*

THE MYSTERY OF MISS OTIS

■ Cole Porter's ballad, 'Miss Otis Regrets', tells the story of a young woman who is betrayed by her lover.

READING SKILLS

Reading aloud

Studying genre

AFTER READING

1 What is the basic storyline of the song? Reduce it to three key points.

2 Why do you think Miss Otis was killed by 'the mob'?

Miss Otis Regrets

Miss Otis regrets she's unable to lunch today, Madam,
Miss Otis regrets she's unable to lunch today,
She is sorry to be delayed,
But last evening down in Lover's Lane she strayed, Madam,
Miss Otis regrets she's unable to lunch today.

When she woke up and found that her dream of love
was gone,
She ran to the man who had led her so far astray,
And from under her velvet gown
She drew a gun and shot her lover down, Madam,
Miss Otis regrets she's unable to lunch today.

When the mob came and got her and dragged her
from the jail, Madam,
They strung her upon the old willow across the way
And the moment before she died,
She lifted up her lovely head and cried, Madam,
Miss Otis regrets she's unable to lunch today.
Miss Otis regrets she's unable to lunch today.

COLE PORTER

■ In this extract from a longer story, Rupert Williams, aged thirteen, takes Cole Porter's song and creates a tale of comedy and intrigue.

The Miss Otis Case

It was just another dreary morning in downtown New York. I sat up to have a look through the half-open window, but slumped back down in my chair. I had one hell of a hangover. The phone purred. I moaned and crawled along the lino. Picking it up, I croaked, 'Franklin speaking'.

'Where the hell have you been Franklin? I've been trying to get you all morning you lazy moron'. It was Fat Al, my boss. I said 'My Aunt in Cincinnati has just had a little girl; I was just wetting her head'.

'By the sound of you, you've drowned her,' Al snapped sarcastically. 'Anyway, get yourself down to the diner for four – I've got some important news for you.

I stuck my tongue out, then slammed down the phone.

Nobody else rang that day so I spent it flicking elastic bands at passing spiders and finishing off a bottle of Gordon's Gin that I had started the previous night.

When I walked into the diner, I saw Fat Al slouched in a chair finishing off a banana split and cappuccino. He beckoned me to come and sit down. 'Well, what's this important news?' I said, Fat Al belched.

'Remember that case last fall about a woman shooting dead her lover?'

'Yep.'

'Well, I think the same thing has happened down in Texas, and I want you on the job.'

I protested, 'I've got five cases I'm working on, Al. I can't possibly leave them now.'

'Name them.' said Al. 'Anyone I know?'

'Well...' I fumbled for names.

'You're on the morning train to Happyville, son,' Al said, with relish. He handed me the ticket. 'Now get out, you lazy jackass.' I left.

My alarm woke me at 7.30 next morning. I cursed and threw it at a fly that was snoozing on my tub of hair shampoo. I fell out of bed and crawled into the shower. I sat on the shower-room floor with my mouth open, catching drops of water, then spitting them out again. The water was far too hot, so I left the shower looking like a lobster, lightly boiled. I showered, dressed, drank, and hurried off to the station.

I was late for the train, but luckily it had been delayed. I

clambered into a smoke-filled, stagnant compartment. US Rail call it second class. I sat beside a lady from Atlanta who spent the first half of the journey telling me about the tomatoes she grew in her backroom. I must have fallen asleep. I was jerked awake by a tall guard looking like a hungry sea-lion who prodded me in the ribs and said; 'Get up, slime. Trying to get a free ride were you?'

'No,' I replied.

'Then get out,' he said triumphantly. I left. Fortunately the train had stopped.

It was sticky and humid outside. I undid my tie and the top button of my shirt. I walked wearily down Main Street, which seemed deserted. I lit a cigarette and watched some kids in the distance chasing each other round a pickup. It was like being in a ghost town. The few people who passed seemed to drift along like phantoms.

I walked to my hotel and pulled a stool up to the bar. 'Straight gin with ice'. I wiped the sweat off my brow and watched the ceiling fan. A man to the right of me started laughing. I turned and looked at him. He was in his early fifties, with a straw hat and torn shirt.

'You New Yorkers certainly can't cope with the south,' he said.

'I have to admit, it is fairly hot,' I replied, to be friendly. He offered his hand.

'Jeff Bakker.'

'Thanks – Nick Franklin'.

'So what's a city-dweller like you doing in a place like this?'

'I'm a P.I.' I said. 'I'm investigating the case of a Miss Jennifer Otis.'

Jeff Bakker sucked his teeth and looked at me. 'Then you're better off going straight home now,' he said. 'I know some pretty ugly people in this town. The last thing they'll want is some cop sniffing around.

I thought for a moment about his words. No harm could come to me could it? After all, I was only doing my job...

RUPERT WILLIAMS

AFTER READING

1 How do you predict this version of the Miss Otis story will develop?

2 Which story elements do you think Rupert Williams handles most successfully - action, description or dialogue? Give examples to support your choice.

COMPARE

Discussion

1 In pairs, read *The Miss Otis Case* aloud, giving as much life to the characterisation as possible. Improvise how the story continues.

2 To write his version of the Miss Otis story, Rupert Williams had to make a number of decisions. Look at the list below and say whether you agree or disagree with what he did:

- setting the story in New York and Texas
- adding a male narrator
- making parts of the story comic
- creating an exaggerated character for Franklin's boss
- keeping visual descriptions of people and places to a minimum

3 How could the Miss Otis story be rewritten to include the same narrator as in the song?

Assignments

1 Read or listen to the song again. Write your own version of the story, this time from the point of view of one of the following characters in the song:

- the narrator in the song
- the addressee (the person who the story is being told to)
- one of the mob

Start by making notes about the character of the person who will tell your story.

2 Choose a song you like which tells a story. Choose a character and tell the story from his or her point of view. Give your readers the words of the song – or a tape of it – so that they can see how you developed the original.

3 Retell Rupert Williams's version of the story from the point of view of Fat Al, Franklin's boss. What new insights into Franklin's personality might we gain?

TRUE CRIME THROUGH THE AGES ═══

■ This section takes a serious look at some real-life crimes from different centuries.

The Murder of the Duke of Buckingham, 23 August 1620

●

The Duke of Buckingham had been James I's favourite, and was a close friend of his son, Charles I. Felton, the assassin, had been refused promotion by the Duke. He pleaded guilty to the murder and was hanged on 27 November 1620.

This day betwixt nine and ten of the clocke in the morning, the Duke of Buckingham, then coming out of a Parlor, into a Hall, to go to his coach and soe to the King (who was four miles off), having about him diverse Lords, Colonells, and Captains, & many of his own Servants was by one Felton (once a Lieutenant of this our Army) slain at one blow, with a dagger knife. In his staggering he turn'd about, uttering onely this word, 'Villaine!' & never spake a word more, but presently plucking out the knife from himself, before he fell to the ground, he made towards the Traytor, two or three paces, and then fell against a Table although he were upheld by diverse that were neare him, that (through the villain's close carriage in the act) could not perceive him hurt at all, but guessed him to be suddenly oversway'd with some apoplexie, till they saw the blood come gushing from his mouth and the wound, soe fast, that life, and breath, at once left his begored body.

You may easily guess what outcries were then made, by us that were Commanders and Officers there present, when once we saw him thus dead in a moment, and slaine by an unknowne hand; for it seems that the Duke himself only knew who it was that had murdered him, and by meanes of the confused presse at the instant about his person, wee neither did nor could. The Souldiers feare his losse will be their utter ruine, wherefore att that instant the house and court about it were full, every man present with the Dukes body, endeavouring a care of itt. In the meane time Felton pass'd the throng, which was confusedly great, not so much as mark'd or followed, in soe much that not knowing where, not who he was that had done that fact, some came to keepe guard at the gates, and others went to the Ramports of the Towne; in all which time the villaine was standing in the kitchin of the same house, and after inquiry made by a multitude of captaines and gentlemen then pressing into the house and court, and crying out a maine 'Where is the villain? Where is the butcher?' he most audaciously and resolutely drawing forth his sword, came out and went amongst them, saying boldly, 'I am the Man, here I am'; upon which diverse drew upon him, with the intent to have dispatcht him; but Sir Thomas Morton, myself, and some others, us'd such means (though with much trouble and difficulty) that we drew him out of their hands, and by order of my Lord High Chamberlaine, wee had the charge of keeping him from any comming to him untill a guard of muskateers were brought, to convey him to the Governor's House, where wee were discharg'd....

But to return to the screeches made att the fatall blow given, the Duchesse of Buckingham and the Countesse of Anglesey came forth into a Gallery which look'd into a Hall where they might behold the blood of their dearest Lord gushing from him; ah, poor Ladies, such was their screechings, teares, and distractions, that I never in my Life heard the like before, and hope never to heare the like againe. His Majesties griefe for the losse of him, was express'd to be more than great, by the many teares hee shed for him, with which I will conclude this sad and untimely News.

Felton had sowed a writing in the crowne of his hatt, half within the lyning, to shew the cause why he putt this cruell act in excution; thinking hee should have been slaine in the place: and it was thus: 'If I bee slaine, let no man condemne me, but rather condemne himself; it is for our sinns that our harts are hardned, and become sencelesse, or else hee had not gone soe long unpunished. John Felton.' 'He is unworthy of the name of a Gentleman, or Soldier, in my opinion, that is afraid to sacrifice his life for the honor of God, his King and Country. John Felton.'

Sir Dudley Carlton

AFTER READING

1 What is the sequence of events in the murder? Write down the key points.

2 How would you describe the narrator's reactions to what he sees?

Murder at Harvard

Until the gray and melancholy twenty-third of November, people of Boston, like most Americans, had been talking all through 1849 of nothing but the great California gold rush. But on that Friday, Boston had something nearer home to occupy its attention. Dr. George Parkman had disappeared in broad daylight. It was as incredible as if Bunker Hill Monument had sunk into the bowels of the earth. A Boston Parkman simply did not, could not, disappear and leave no trace. The police went to work, and so did hundreds of citizens, spurred by a reward of $3000 for the doctor, alive or dead.

That day the eminent doctor had left his Beacon Hill home about noon. He had gone to the Merchants' Bank. From there he had called at a greengrocer's to leave an order. Later he had been seen walking rapidly toward Harvard Medical College. At or near the college, it appeared, he had walked straight into Valhalla.

It was Dr. Parkman who had given the very land on which the then new Medical College stood. Moreover, he had endowed the Parkman Chair of Anatomy, occupied by Dr. Oliver Wendell Holmes. The Parkmans had been prominent from what, even by Boston standards, were ancient times. All the Parkmans were well-to-do; the doctor was so wealthy that his son, who never earned a penny in his life, was able to leave $5,000,000 for the improvement of Boston Common. The usually staid Boston press went into a dither and police arrested scores of persons.

Professor John White Webster made a call on the missing man's brother, and said that he had had an interview with the doctor in the Medical College on Friday afternoon, at which time he had paid Dr. Parkman $483. Dr. Parkman had then left the college, said the professor.

Webster, a graduate of Harvard Medical, had taught chemistry at Harvard for more than twenty years. With their four pretty daughters, the Websters were noted for the hospitality they lavished on the faculty. His professor's salary of $1200 annually was wholly inadequate. While it was known that Webster owed the doctor money and that the doctor had gone to collect it, the professor was not under suspicion. Who could suspect a faculty member of Harvard? It began to look as if some thug had waylaid the doctor, done away with him and made off with the $483 which Webster said he had paid Parkman.

Apparently nobody suspected Webster – except a morose and obscure man named Ephraim Littlefield, a janitor at Harvard Medical College. It appears to have been a generous act of Webster's that set Littlefield on his trail like a hound of hell. On the Tuesday following Parkman's disappearance, Webster presented a thumping big turkey to Littlefield – the first gift the janitor had received in seven years of work at the college. Littlefield not only brooded over the gift, but he was troubled because talk on the street had it that 'they'll sure find Dr. Parkman's body somewhere in the Medical College'. Medical colleges in those days were held to be notorious receivers of the products of professional body snatchers.

'I got tired', said Littlefield in explaining his next move, 'of all that talk'. Accordingly, into his dismal basement apartment at the college he lugged drills, hammers, chisels, crowbars. He told his startled wife that he was going to dig through the brick vault under Professor Webster's laboratory room. Mrs Littlefield was dreadfully frightened; suspicion of a Harvard professor was an act against nature, perhaps even against God.

A few days before Parkman's disappearance, the janitor explained to her, he was helping Webster in his laboratory. Suddenly Dr Parkman appeared before them. 'Webster,' he cried, 'are you ready for me tonight?' Webster replied: 'No, I am not ready tonight'. Parkman shook his cane. 'Webster.' he said savagely, 'something must be accomplished tomorrow.' Then he left.

For the next several days, Littlefield had brooded and wondered whether on the next call Professor Webster *had* been ready. 'And *now*,' said the janitor to his wife, 'what do you think?'

So on Thanksgiving Day, while the turkey sputtered in the oven, he hammered and drilled his way into the solid brick wall. Progress was slow, but Littlefield was as determined as he was suspicious. At noon he refreshed himself with the great bird and cranberries, then returned to his labours. He continued his work on Friday, after his regular duties, and that night broke through. 'I held my light forward,' he related, 'and the first thing I saw was the pelvis of a man and two parts of a leg. I knew,' he added darkly, 'this was no place for such things.'

Littlefield called the police. Within a short time Webster was in a cell of the city jail. Next day the press and the town went delirious. 'Horrible suspicions!!' screamed the normally sedate Transcript. 'Arrest of Professor J. W. Webster!' Harvard College and Beacon Hill seemed about to tumble into the Charles River.

Professor Webster was put on trial on the nineteenth of March, 1850. The state's star witness, janitor Littlefield, took the stand and his testimony was bad indeed for the professor. The defence presented a long and distinguished array of character and other witnesses. President Sparks of Harvard thought Webster 'kind and humane'. Nathaniel Bowditch, son of the celebrated mathematician, believed Webster to be 'irritable though kind-hearted'. Oliver Wendell Holmes testified both for the defence and the state. For the latter, he said that whoever had cut up the body alleged to be that of Dr. Parkman had certainly been handy with surgical knives.

The state was attempting to prove that the remnants of human mortality discovered in the vault – and in the laboratory stove – were those of Dr. Parkman; and the defence was doing its best to prove the fragments to have been almost anybody but Dr. Parkman. Day after day the trial continued and much of Boston sought to get into the courtroom. The marshal cleared the visitors' gallery every ten minutes, thus permitting thousands of persons to witness portions of the event of the century.

Slowly the coils closed around Professor Webster; and late on the eleventh day the jury was charged by Chief Justice Lemuel Shaw in an address which is still considered by lawyers to be one of the great expositions of all time on the subject of circumstantial evidence. Three hours later the jury returned a verdict of guilty.

Long before Professor Webster was hanged on August 30, 1850, he made a confession. On that fatal Friday, Parkman had called Webster a scoundrel and furiously shaken his cane in the professor's face. Then, said Webster, 'I felt nothing but the sting of his words, and in my fury I seized a stick of wood and dealt him a blow with all the force that passion could give it.' One blow was enough. Parkman fell, bleeding at the mouth. Webster bolted the doors, stripped the dead man, hoisted him into the sink and then dismembered him with the deft professional strokes that had been admired by Dr. Holmes.

The painful celebrity that came to Harvard has been dissipated in the century that has intervened, but more than one member of the faculty long felt the blight cast by Professor Webster. Bliss Perry once related how his mother, at Williamstown, Massachusetts, refused to entertain a Harvard professor who had come there, some twenty years after the crime, as a delegate to a convention of New England college officials. Mrs. Perry vowed firmly that she could not sleep 'if one of those Harvard professors was in the house'. The professor who had to find quarters elsewhere was James Russell Lowell.

Another incident concerns the lawyer (later the Union general) Ben Butler, to whom Harvard had somehow neglected to grant an LL.D. While he was cross-examining a witness in court, and treating him rather roughly, the judge intervened to remind Butler that the witness was no less than a Harvard professor. 'Yes, I know, Your Honour,' said Ben. 'We hanged one the other day.'

Professor Webster's fame is secure. He remains the only Harvard professor to have performed lethally while a member of the faculty, and the sole college professor to gain entrance to the chaste pages of the Dictionary of American Biography on the strength of his stout right arm.

STUART H HOLBROOK

AFTER READING

1 What do we learn about the character of Dr Webster? Try and find five main details.

2 Apart from the dates given, how can you tell that this extract is describing a past event?

HANDCARVED COFFINS
BY TRUMAN CAPOTE

A Nonfiction Account of an American Crime

March, 1975.
A town in a small Western state. A focus for the many large farms and cattle-raising ranches surrounding it, the town, with a population of less than ten thousand, supports twelve churches and two restaurants. A movie house, though it has not shown a movie in ten years, still stands stark and cheerless on Main Street. There once was a hotel, too; but that also has been closed, and nowadays the only place a traveller can find shelter is the Prairie Motel.

The motel is clean, the rooms are well heated; that's about all you can say for it. A man named Jake Pepper has been living there for almost five years. He is fifty-eight, a widower with four grown sons. He is five-foot-ten, in top condition, and looks fifteen years younger than his age. He has a handsome-homely face with periwinkle blue eyes and a thin mouth that twitches into quirky shapes that are sometimes smiles and sometimes not. The secret of his boyish appearance is not his lanky trimness, not his chunky ripe-apple cheeks, not his naughty mysterious grins; it's because of his hair that he looks like somebody's kid brother: dark blond, clipped short, and so afflicted with cowlicks that he cannot really comb it; he sort of wets it down.

Jake Pepper is a detective employed by the State Bureau of Investigation. We had first met each other through a close mutual friend, another detective in a different state. In 1972 he wrote a letter saying he was working on a murder case, something that he thought might interest me. I telephoned him and we talked for three hours. I was very interested in what he had to tell me, but he became alarmed when I suggested that I travel out there and survey the situation myself; he said that would be premature and might endanger his investigation, but he promised to keep me informed. For the next three years we exchanged telephone calls every few months. The case, developing along lines intricate as a rat's maze, seemed to have reached an impasse. Finally I said: Just let me come there and look around.

And so it was that I found myself one cold March night sitting with Jake Pepper in his motel room on the wintry, windblown outskirts of this forlorn little Western town. Actually, the room was pleasant, cosy; after all, off and on, it had been Jake's home for almost five years, and he had built shelves to display pictures of his family, his sons and grandchildren, and to hold hundreds of books, many of them concerning the Civil War and all of them the selections of an intelligent man: he was partial to Dickens, Melville, Trollope, Mark Twain.

Jake sat crosslegged on the floor, a glass of bourbon beside him. He had a chessboard spread before him: absently he shifted the chessmen about.

TRUMAN CAPOTE: The amazing thing is, nobody seems to know anything about this case. It's had almost no publicity.

JAKE: There are reasons.

TC: I've never been able to put it into proper sequence. It's like a jigsaw puzzle with half the pieces missing.

JAKE: Where shall we begin?

TC: From the beginning.

JAKE: Go over to the bureau. Look in the bottom drawer. See that little cardboard box? Take a look at what's inside it.

(What I found inside the box was a miniature coffin. It was a beautifully made object, carved from light balsam wood. It was undecorated: but when one opened the hinged lid one discovered the coffin was not empty. It contained a photograph - a casual, candid snapshot of two middle-aged people, a man and a woman, crossing a street. It was not a posed picture; one sensed that the subjects were unaware that they were being photographed.)

That little coffin. I guess that's what you might call the beginning.

TC: And the picture?

JAKE: George Roberts and his wife. George and Amelia Roberts.

TC: Mr and Mrs Roberts. Of course. The first victims. He was a lawyer?

JAKE: He was a lawyer, and one morning (to be exact: the tenth of August 1970) he got a present in the mail. That little coffin. With the picture inside it. Roberts was a happy-go-lucky guy: he showed it to some people around the court-house and acted like it was a joke. One month later George and Amelia were two very dead people.

TC: How soon did you come on the case?

JAKE: Immediately. An hour after they found them I was on my way here with two other agents from the Bureau. When we got here the bodies were still in the car. And so were the snakes. That's something I'll never forget. Never.

TC: Go back. Describe it exactly.

JAKE: The Robertses had no children. Nor enemies, either. Everybody liked them. Amelia worked for her husband; she was his secretary. They had only one car, and they always drove to work together. The morning it happened was hot. A sizzler. So I guess they must have been surprised when they went out to get in their car and found all the windows rolled up. Anyway, they each entered the car through separate doors, and as soon as they were inside – *wam*! A tangle of rattlesnakes hit them like lightning. We found nine rattlers inside that car. All of them had been injected with amphetamine; they were crazy, they bit the Robertses everywhere; neck, arms, ears, cheeks, hands. Poor people. Their heads were huge and swollen like Halloween pumpkins painted green. They must have died almost instantly. I hope so. That's one hope I really hope.

TC: Rattlesnakes aren't that prevalent in these regions. Not rattlesnakes of that calibre. They must have been brought here.

JAKE: They were. From a snake farm in Nogales, Texas. But now's not the time to tell you how I know that.

(Outside, crusts of snow laced the ground; spring was a long way off - a hard wind whipping the window announced that winter was still with us. But the sound of the wind was only a murmur in my head underneath the racket of rattling rattlesnakes, hissing tongues. I saw the car dark under a hot sun, the swirling serpents, the human heads growing green, expanding with poison. I listened to the wind, letting it wipe the scene away.')

JAKE: 'Course, we don't know if the Baxters ever got a coffin. I'm sure they did; it wouldn't fit the pattern if they hadn't. But they never mentioned receiving a coffin, and we never found a trace of it.

TC: Perhaps it got lost in the fire. But wasn't there someone with them, another couple?

JAKE: The Hogans. From Tulsa. They were just friends of the Baxters who were passing through. The killer never meant to kill them. It was just an accident.

See, what happened was: the Baxters were building a fancy new house, but the only part of it that was really finished was the basement. All the rest was still under construction. Roy Baxter was a well-to-do man; he could've afforded to rent this whole motel while his house was being built. But he chose to live in this underground basement, and the only entrance to it was through a trap door.

It was December – three months after the rattlesnake murders. All we know for certain is: the Baxters invited this couple from Tulsa to spend the night with them in their basement. And some time just before dawn one humdinger of a fire broke out in the basement, and the four people were incinerated. I mean that literally: burnt to ashes.

TC: But couldn't they have escaped through the trap door?

JAKE (twisting his lips, snorting): Hell, no. The arsonist, the murderer, had piled cement blocks on top of it. King Kong couldn't have budged it.

TC: But obviously there had to be some connection between the fire and the rattlesnakes.

JAKE: That's easy to say now. But damned if I could make any connection. We had five guys working this case; we knew more about George and Amelia Roberts, about the Baxters and the Hogans, than they ever knew about themselves. I'll bet George Roberts never knew his wife had a baby when she was fifteen and had given it away for adoption.

'Course, in a place this size, everybody more or less knows everybody else, at least by sight. But we could find nothing that linked the victims. Or any motivations. There was no reason, none that we could find, why anybody would want to kill any of those people. (He studied his chessboard; he lit a pipe and sipped his bourbon.) The victims, all of them were strangers to me. I'd never heard of them till they were dead. But the next fellow was a friend of mine. Clem Anderson. Second generation Norwegian; he'd inherited a ranch here from his father, a pretty nice spread. We'd gone to college together, though he was a freshman when I was a senior. He married an old girl-friend of mine, wonderful girl, the only girl I've ever seen with lavender eyes. Like amethyst. Sometimes, when I'd had a snootful, I used to talk about Amy and her amethyst eyes, and my wife didn't think it was one bit funny. Anyway, Clem and Amy got married and settled out here and had seven children. I had dinner at their house the night before he got killed, and Amy said the only regret she had in life was that she hadn't had more children.

But I'd been seeing a lot of Clem right along. Ever since I came out here on the case. He had a wild streak, he drank too much; but he was shrewd, he taught me a lot about this town.

One night he called me here at the motel. He sounded funny. He said he had to see me right away. So I said come on over. I thought he was drunk, but it wasn't that – he was scared. Know why?

TC: Santa Claus had sent him a present.

JAKE: Uh-huh. But you see, he didn't know what it was. What it meant. The coffin, and its possible connection to the rattlesnake murders, had never been made public. We were keeping that a secret. I had never mentioned the matter to Clem.

So when he arrived in this very room, and showed me a coffin that was an exact replica of the one the Robertses had received, I knew my friend was in great danger. It had been mailed to him in a box wrapped in brown paper; his name and address were printed in an anonymous style. Black ink.

TC: And was there a picture of him?

JAKE: Yes. And I'll describe it carefully because it is very relevant to the manner of Clem's death. Actually, I think the murderer meant it as a little joke, a sly hint as to how Clem was going to die.

In the picture, Clem is seated in a kind of jeep. An eccentric vehicle of his own invention. It had no top and it had no windshield, nothing to protect the driver at all. It was just an engine with four wheels. He said he'd never seen the picture before, and had no idea who had taken it or when.

Now I had a difficult decision. Should I confide in him, admit that the Roberts family had received a similar coffin before their deaths, and that the Baxters probably had as well? In some ways it might be better not to inform him: that way, if we kept close surveillance, he might lead us to the killer, and do it more easily by not being aware of his danger.

TC: But you decided to tell him.

JAKE: I did. Because, with this second coffin in hand, I was certain the murders were connected. And I felt that Clem must know the answer. He *must*.

But after I explained the significance of the coffin, he went into shock. I had to slap his face. And then he was like a child: he lay down on the bed and began to cry: 'Somebody's going to kill me. Why? Why?' I told him: 'Nobody's going to kill you. I can promise you that. But *think*, Clem! What do you have in common with these people who *did* die? There must be something. Maybe something very trivial.' But all he could say was: 'I don't know, I don't know.' I forced him to drink until he was drunk enough to fall asleep. He spend the night here. In the morning he was calmer. But he still could not think of anything that connected him with the crimes, see how he in any way fitted into a pattern. I told him not to discuss the coffin with anyone, not even his wife; and I told him not to worry – I was importing an extra two agents just to keep an eye on him.

TC: And how long was it before the coffin-maker kept his promise?

JAKE: Oh, I think he must have been enjoying it. He teased it along like a fisherman with a trout trapped in a bowl. The Bureau recalled the extra agents, and finally even Clem seemed to shrug it off. Six months went by. Amy called and invited me out to dinner. A warm summer night. The air was full of fireflies. Some of the children chased about catching them and putting them into jars.

As I was leaving, Clem walked me out to my car. A narrow river ran along the path where it was parked, and Clem said: 'About that connection business. The other day I suddenly thought of something. The river.' I said what river; and he said that river, the one flowing past us. 'It's kind of a complicated story. And probably silly. But I'll tell you the next time I see you.'

Of course I never saw him again. At least, not alive.

TRUMAN CAPOTE

AFTER READING

1 What do you think the connection with the river could be?

2 How does Truman Capote build a sense of tension?

COMPARE

Discussion

1 Try to summarise the content of each extract in a single sentence. What problems do you encounter? Which text is most difficult to summarise? Why?

2 Each of these extracts describes true events. Yet some have the feel of fictional stories. Which account is:
- most factual
- most descriptive
- most uninteresting
- most gripping?

Support your ideas with specific examples.

3 Pick out three key words from each extract which show the age in which they were written, i.e. seventeenth century, nineteenth century and twentieth century. Compare your choices with others in the group.

Assignments

1 Take Truman Capote's account and continue it, describing what you think happens next. Try to imitate his style of writing, or the style of one of the other two pieces.

2 Many people believe that crime is glamorised too much.

> Programmes on television recreate real-life crimes, making us all more nervous about living in a violent world, and making unexpected heroes of the villains.

How far do you agree with this opinion? Do you think these programmes are irresponsible?

Write a speech or an essay expressing your point of view on this issue.

CRIME AND PUNISHMENT ≡≡≡≡

■ This section gives you tables of statistics and results of opinion polls to help you compare crime figures in this country with crime elsewhere in the world.

COUNTRIES WHICH HAVE ABOLISHED THE DEATH PENALTY SINCE 1976

1976	Portugal*; Canada**
1978	Denmark*; Spain**
1979	Luxembourg, Nicaragua, Norway*; Brazil(1), Fiji, Peru**
1981	France*
1982	The Netherlands*
1983	Cyprus, El Salvador**
1984	Argentina(2), Australia*
1985	Australia*
1987	The Philippines, Haiti, Liechtenstein, German Democratic Republic*
1989	Cambodia, New Zealand, Romania*
1990	Andorra, Czech and Slovak Federative Republic, Hungary, Ireland, Mozambique, Namibia, São Tomé and Principe*; Nepal**(3)

* for all offences **for ordinary offences

1   Brazil had abolished the death penalty in 1882 but reintroduced it in 1969 while under military rule.
2. Argentina had abolished the death penalty for all offences in 1921 and again in 1972 but reintroduced it in 1976 following a military coup.
3. Nepal had abolished the death penalty for murder in 1946 but reintroduced it in 1985 after bomb explosions killed several people.

HIGHEST SENTENCES 1990

judicial area	murder	rape
Canada	life	life
Denmark	life	3 years
England and Wales	life	15 years
Greece	life	20 years
Hong Kong	death	life
India	death	10 years
Republic of Ireland	life	18 months
Kenya	death	life
Netherlands	life	5 years
New Zealand	life	6 years
Nigeria	death	life
Norway	21 years	5 years

judicial area		
Scotland	life	10 years
Spain	30 years	20 years
United Arab Emirates	death	life
Texas	death	50 years

judicial area	severe *assault*	*tax fraud*
Canada	4 years	18 months
Denmark	1 year	10 months
England and Wales	5 years	3 years
Greece	5 years	5 years
Hong Kong	3 years	3 years
India	1 year	n/a
Republic of Ireland	suspended sentence	repayment
Kenya	life	3 years
Netherlands	2 years	1 year
New Zealand	4 years	large fine
Nigeria	7 years	7 years
Norway	18 months	6 months
Scotland	5 years	3 years
Spain	6 years	6 years
United Arab Emirates	5 years	n/a
Texas	10 years	99 years

judicial area	*armed robbery*	*soft drugs (possession)*
Canada	5 years	n/a
Denmark	6 years	fine
England and Wales	14 years	1 year
Greece	20 years	1 year
Hong Kong	life	life
India	7 years	n/a
Republic of Ireland	5 years	n/a
Kenya	death	n/a
Netherlands	6 years	n/a
New Zealand	9 years	n/a
Nigeria	death	21 years
Norway	2 years	n/a
Scotland	10 years	18 months
Spain	6 years	4 years
United Arab Emirates	life	10 years
Texas	99 years	1 year

OPINIONS OF POLICE POWERS - SURVEY

Do you think the police should or should not have the power to do the following things?

	Should	Should not	Don't know
Fingerprint everyone in an area where a serious crime has been committed?	65	31	4
Question suspects before they have been allowed to consult a lawyer?	34	59	7
Stop and search anyone they think is suspicious?	55	40	4
Detain suspects for more than 24 hours without charging them?	29	63	9
Have access to files containing information on citizens who don't have a criminal record?	15	81	4
Use plastic bullets, water canon and teargas to disperse potentially violent demonstrators?	61	33	6
Tap telephones and record private conversations?	15	78	7
Carry firearms at all times, as in America and some continental countries?	22	72	6

HUTCHINSON GALLUP INFO 92

AFTER READING

1 Which country is most severe on both murder and tax fraud?

2 Which country is most severe on both armed robbery and soft drugs?

3 Which country seems in general harshest and which most lenient?

Discussion

1 Discuss with your partner what the asterisks indicate in the Death Penalty table, i.e. what do you imagine the difference is between 'all offences' and 'ordinary offences'?

2 Do most British people, according to the survey, support the police? Do most want to see police powers increased?

3 What, if anything, do you find surprising about the answers given in the two surveys?

Assignments

1 What do you have a strong opinion about? In pairs, or small groups, think of five questions about this subject to create a survey. Then ask the rest of the class to answer your questions.

2 How could the data have been better presented, so that information was easier to find? Write a paragraph outlining your ideas.

WIDER READING

Detective Fiction

Many books are written in this genre. Here are a few recommended titles:

Ruth Rendell, *Heartstones*; Pateman and Sidney, *Crimebusters* (short stories); Agatha Christie, *A Murder is Announced*; Ngaio Marsh, *Tied up in Tinsel*; Sara Paretsky, *Indemnity Only*; Jessica Mann, *Death Beyond the Nile*.

Real-life Crime

Richard Glyn Jones, *The Giant Book of True Crime*; Truman Capote, *Music for Chameleons*; Tom Wolfe (ed), *The New Journalism*; John Carey, *The Faber Book of Reportage*; Geoff Barton, *Reportage*.

AFTER READING

1 From your reading of detective fiction, write about two characters who particularly interest you. Compare and contrast their attitudes and reactions to crime.

2 Write an introduction to a collection of crime stories, discussing why you think people are so fascinated by the theme.

TO WHOM IT MAY CONCERN

It is widely believed that the art of writing letters is dead. Nowadays, it is much quicker, and simpler, to pick up the telephone or to send a fax. However, it could be argued that there are still some forms of communication that are best suited to the letter.
- *When are letters the best way of communicating?*
- *Could you send a love fax?*
- *What is the best way to make a complaint?*

EXPRESS YOURSELF

■ People often find it very difficult to write letters explaining a complicated event to someone who wasn't there at the time. The following writers certainly appear to find it difficult to present their sides of the story effectively.

READING SKILLS

Analysing language

Business Letters

It's not only what you say, but how you say it that matters. Letters of complaint are fraught with difficulty. You have to present your point of view clearly in order to appear reasonable. Judge for yourself how effective these extracts are. They are genuine extracts from letters sent to the Council and to an insurance company.

LETTERS TO THE COUNCIL

I wish to complain that my father hurt his back very badly when he put his foot in the hole in the back passage.

The toilet seat is cracked. Where do I stand?

I am writing on behalf of my sink which is running away from the wall.

I request your permission to remove my drawers in the kitchen.

Will you please send someone to mend our broken path. Yesterday my wife tripped on it and is now pregnant.

When I applied for a rebate you said that you would have to take something off. Now that you have taken it off, I have been told that you should have put some on. So will you please take off what you took off and put on what you should.

LETTERS TO THE INSURANCE COMPANY

Coming home I drove into the wrong house and collided with a tree that I don't have.

I thought my window was down, but I found out it was up when I put my head through it.

The guy was all over the road. I had to swerve a number of times before I hit him.

In an attempt to kill a fly I drove into a telegraph pole.

An invisible car came out of nowhere, struck my car and vanished.

The indirect cause of the accident was a little guy in a small car with a big mouth.

I saw a slow-moving, sad-faced old gentleman as he bounced off the roof of my car.

I had been driving for forty years when I fell asleep at the wheel and had an accident.

■ The following are actual details from letters in which car drivers were trying to summarise the details of their car accidents.

AFTER READING

1 Working in pairs, try to decipher what the writers of each of the complaints actually meant when they wrote the letter.

2 Choose three of four of the sentences in which strange use of language has obscured the meaning. Analyse exactly where the writer has gone wrong.

■ The writers of the letters to the council and to the insurance company certainly had some difficulty in making their case effectively. Read the next two letters carefully. Both are on the same topic, the wearing of school uniform. Both letter writers think that school uniform is a bad idea, but they choose different ways to put across the points that they want to make.

> ### READING SKILLS
> Analysing language

Letters to the Head

Dear Headteacher,

As a pupil of this school, I am sure that you will agree that I have the right to write about a subject that affects me, and that is the subject of school uniform.

I believe that school children should not have to wear school uniform for the following reasons:

Britain is the only country in Europe that enforces the wearing of school uniform. Pupils in European countries are allowed to wear their own clothes for school. This does not seem to make them badly behaved or to affect their ability to learn. In fact, standards of education in France, where pupils wear their own comfortable clothes, seem to be higher than those in England.

A great deal of time in school that should be spent on teaching and learning is wasted in futile arguments between teachers and pupils over the issue of school uniform. I think that there would be a better relationship between teachers and pupils if teachers did not have to tell pupils off constantly about wearing non-uniform clothes. This would also allow more time for the teachers to teach and the pupils to learn!

School uniform is uncomfortable and impractical. It is also very expensive. Some parents find it difficult to pay for the regulation school blazer and the many other items (including P.E. kits) that pupils are expected to have.

If you do not feel that you could allow a totally free choice of clothes, would you consider relaxing the uniform regulations so that pupils could, within certain guidelines (e.g. no jeans), choose the clothes that they want to wear to school? This would stop certain pupils going too far and wearing outrageous clothes in school.

I hope that you will consider seriously the points that I have put forward in this letter.

Dear Headteacher

I do not think that I should have to wear school uniform. I would like to wear jeans and trainers to school as I am more comfortable in these clothes.

Also I do not like the colour of the school uniform. I would prefer it to be purple and green, rather than black.

I work better at home when I am wearing my own clothes than I do at school when I am wearing my school uniform. Working at home I don't get annoyed by the itchy collars of school shirts and the heavy school blazers which are too hot in the summer and too cold in the winter. I would definitely learn more if I could wear my own clothes to school!

AFTER READING

1 Which of the two letters do you think would influence the headteacher more? Give reasons for your view.

COMPARE

Discussion

1 With your partner, compare the styles of the following sentences:

As a pupil of this school, I am sure that you will agree that I have the right to write about a subject that affects me, and that is the subject of school uniform.

Also I do not like the colour of the school uniform.

2 With a partner examine the language used in each letter. Take into account the following points:
- the vocabulary that each letter writer uses
- the way in which the writer of each letter backs up his or her points with examples.

Assignments

1 Are there any other arguments for the abolition of school uniform that the writers of the letters have missed? What are they?

2 Working in pairs, make a list of the arguments that could be made for the wearing of school uniform. Then decide what your views are on this issue.

3 Write your own letter to the Headteacher expressing your opinions about the subject of school uniform. Do you want to keep it as it is? Is there anything about your school uniform that you would want to change? Do you think that it should be abolished altogether?

SISTERLY LOVE

■ These two letters form part of an incomplete novel, *Love and Friendship*, which was written in the eighteenth century by the fifteen-year-old Jane Austen.

In the novel, Mary Stanhope and her sister Georgiana write to their friends about a proposal of marriage.

Miss Stanhope to Mrs...

My Dear Fanny

I am the happiest creature in the World, for I have received an offer of marriage from Mr Watts. It is the first I have ever had & I hardly know how to value it enough. How I will triumph over the Duttons! I do not intend to accept it, at least I believe not, but as I am not quite certain I gave him an equivocal answer & left him. And now my dear Fanny I want your Advice whether I should accept his offer or not, but that you may be able to judge of his merits & the situation of affairs I will give you an account of them. He is quite an old Man, about two & thirty, very plain, *so* plain that I cannot bear to look at him. He is extremely disagreeable & I hate him more than any body else in the world. He has a large fortune & will make great Settlements on me; but then he is very healthy. In short I do not know what to do. If I refuse him he as good as told me that he should offer himself to Sophia and if she refused him to Georgiana, & I could not bear to have either of them married before me. If I accept him I know I shall be miserable all the rest of my Life, for he is very ill tempered & peevish extremely jealous, & so stingy that there is no living in the house with him. He told me he should mention the affair to Mama, but I insisted upon it that he did not for very likely she would make me marry him whether I would or no; however probably he *has* before now, for he never does anything he is desired to do. I believe I shall have him. It will be such a triumph to be married before Sophy, Georgiana & the Duttons; And he promised to have a new Carriage on the occasion, but we almost quarrelled about the colour, for I insisted upon its being blue spotted with silver, & he declared it should be a plain Chocolate; & to provoke me more said it should be just as low as his old one. I wont have him I declare. He said he should come again tomorrow & take my final answer, so I believe I must get him while I can. I know the Duttons will envy me & I shall be able to chaprone Sophy & Georgiana to all the Winter Balls. But then what will be the use of that when very likely he wont let me go myself for I know he hates dancing & has a great idea of Womens never going from home. What he hates himself he has no idea of any other person's liking; & besides he talks a great deal of Women's always staying at home & such stuff. I believe I shant have him; I would refuse him at once if I were certain that neither of my Sisters would accept him & that if they did not, he would not offer to the Duttons. I cannot run such a risk, so, if he will promise to have the Carriage ordered as I like, I will have him, if not he may ride in it by himself for me. I hope you like my determination; I can think of nothing better;

And am your ever Affecte

Mary Stanhope

AFTER READING

1 Make a list of the reasons that Mary Stanhope gives for marrying Mr Watts. Are these good reasons for getting married?

2 What do you learn about Mary's character by reading this letter?

BEFORE READING

In this box is an extract from the next letter that you will read. In it, Georgiana, Mary's youngest sister, is writing to her friend Anne. She tells her about the decision that Mary has to make – whether she should accept or refuse Mr Watts's proposal. Write down what you think are the missing words. Then compare your version with the one written by Jane Austen:

Miss Georgiana Stanhope to Miss xxx

Our neighbour Mr Watts has made proposals to Mary: Proposals which she knew not how to receive for tho' she has a particular .... to him (in which she is not singular) yet she would willingly .... him sooner that risk his .... to Sophy or me which in case of a refusal from herself, he told her he should do, for you must know the .... Girl considers our marrying before her as one of the greatest .... that can possibly befall her, and to prevent it would willingly ensure herself everlasting .... by a .... with Mr Watts.

My Dear Anne

Sophy & I have just been practising a little deceit on our eldest Sister, to which we are not perfectly reconciled, & yet the circumstances were such that if any thing will excuse it, they must. Our neighbour Mr Watts has made proposals to Mary: Proposals which she knew not how to receive for tho' she has a particular Dislike to him (in which she is not singular) yet she would willingly marry him sooner than risk his offering to Sophy or me which in case of a refusal from herself, he told her he should do, for you must know the poor Girl considers our marrying before her as one of the greatest misfortunes that can possibly befall her, & to prevent it would willingly ensure herself everlasting Misery by a Marriage with Mr Watts. An hour ago she came to us to sound our inclinations respecting the affair which were to determine hers. A little before she came my Mother had given us an account of it, telling us that she certainly would not let him go farther than our own family for a Wife. "And therefore (said she) If Mary won't have him Sophy must, & if Sophy wont Georgiana *shall*". Poor

Georgiana! – We neither of us attempted to alter my Mother's resolution, which I am sorry to say is generally more strictly kept than rationally formed. As soon as she was gone however I broke silence to assure Sophy that if Mary should refuse Mr Watts I should not expect her to sacrifice *her* happiness by becoming his Wife from a motive of Generosity to me, which I was afraid her Good nature & sisterly affection might induce her to do.

"Let us flatter ourselves (replied She) that Mary will not refuse him. Yet how can I hope that my Sister may accept a Man who cannot make her happy."

"*He* cannot it is true but his Fortune, his Name, his House, his Carriage will and I have no doubt but that Mary will marry him; indeed why should she not? he is not more than two & thirty; a very proper age for a Man to marry at; He is rather plain to be sure, but then what is Beauty in a Man; if he has but a genteel figure & a sensible-looking Face it is quite sufficient."

"This is all very true Georgiana but Mr Watt's figure is unfortunately extremely vulgar & and his Countenance is very heavy."

"And then as to his temper; it has been reckoned bad, but may not the World be deceived in their Judgement of it. There is an open Frankness in his Disposition which becomes a Man; They say he is stingy; We'll call that Prudence. They say he is suspicious. *That* proceeds from a warmth of Heart always excusable in Youth, & in short I see no reason why he should not make a very good Husband, or why Mary should not be very happy with him."

Sophy laughed; I continued,

"However whether Mary accepts him or not I am resolved. My determination is made. I never would marry Mr Watts were Beggary the only alternative. So deficient in every respect! Hideous in his person and without one good Quality to make amends for it. His fortune to be sure is good. Yet not so very large! Three thousand a year. What is three thousand a year? It is but six times as much as my Mother's income. It will not tempt me."

"Yet it will be a noble fortune for Mary" said Sophy laughing again.

"For Mary! Yes indeed it will give me pleasure to see *her* in such affluence."

Thus I ran on to the great Entertainment of my Sister till Mary came into the room to appearance in great agitation. She sate down. We made room for her at the fire. She seemed at a loss how to begin & and at last said in some confusion

"Pray Sophy have you any mind to be married?"

"To be married! None in the least. But why do you ask me? Are you acquainted with any one who means to make me proposals?"

"I – no, how should I? But mayn't I ask a common question?"

"Not a very *common* one Mary surely" (said I). She paused & after some moments silence went on – "How should you like to marry Mr Watts, Sophy?"

I winked at Sophy & replied for her. "Who is there but must rejoice to marry a man of three thousand a year who keeps a postchaise & pair, with silver Harness, a boot & a window to look out at behind?"

"Very true (she replied). That's very true. So you would have him if he would offer, Georgiana, & would *you* Sophy?"

Sophy did not like the idea of telling a lie & deceiving her Sister; she prevented the first & saved half her conscience by equivocation. "I should certainly act just as Georgiana would do."

"Well then said Mary with triumph in her Eyes, *I* have had an offer from Mr Watts."

We were of course very much surprised; "Oh! do not accept him" said I, "and then perhaps he may have me."

In short my scheme took & Mary is resolved to do that to prevent our supposed happiness which she would not have done to ensure it in reality. Yet after all my Heart cannot acquit me & Sophy is even more scrupulous. Quiet our Minds my dear Anne by writing & telling us you approve our conduct. Consider it well over. Mary will have real pleasure in being a married Woman, & able to chaprone us, which she certainly shall do, for I think myself bound to contribute as much as possible to her happiness in a State I have made her choose. They will probably have a new Carriage, which will be paradise to her, & if we can prevail on Mr. W. to set up his Phaeton she will be too happy. These things however would be no consolation to Sophy or me for domestic Misery. Remember all this & do not condemn us.

JANE AUSTEN

AFTER READING

1 How did Georgiana and Sophy trick Mary into marrying Mr Watts?

2 What would you have done if you were in their situation?

COMPARE

Discussion

1 With a partner, discuss and choose one word or phrase to describe Mary, one for Georgiana and one for Sophy. Give reasons for your choice.

2 Look again at Georgiana's letter. Working in groups of two or three, practise reading aloud the conversation between Mary and her sisters. First analyse the girls' feelings (deceit, guilt surprise, triumph, etc) and try to convey these during the reading.

3 At the end of her letter, Georgiana writes: "Quiet our minds my dear Anne by writing and telling us you approve our conduct." Discuss whether you do or do not approve of the way that Georgiana and Sophy have treated Mary. Then write the reply that you think Anne might have written to Georgiana.

Assignments

1 Read through Mary's and Georgiana's letters, making notes about Mr Watts. Using these notes, write your own description of Mr Watts's appearance and character. Would he be a good husband?

2 In pairs, make a list of the words and phrases used in the conversation between Mary and her sisters which would not be used, or would be used differently, today. Then give a modern equivalent for each word or phrase that you have chosen. Set out your list like this:

Words and phrases	Modern equivalents
Sound our inclinations	Ask our opinions

4 Rewrite the conversation between Mary and her sisters in modern English.

LETTERS FROM AMERICA

■ Letter writers can have very important and powerful things to say. These two letters raise issues that are very relevant in today's world. Both these writers seem to have had the ability to see something of the future in their present.

Chief Seattle was the leader of the Dwamish, Suquamish and allied Indian tribes. This letter was written in reply to a request that the chief sell the Native Americans' lands to the white settlers.

READING SKILLS
Reading for meaning
Analysing language
Developing personal response

Chief Seattle to the President of the United States, 1854

How can you buy or sell the sky, the warmth of the land? The idea is strange to us.

If we do not own the freshness of the air and the sparkle of the water, how can you buy them?

Every part of this earth is sacred to my people.

Every shining pine needle, every sandy shore, every mist in the dark woods, every clearing and humming insect is holy in the memory and experience of my people. The sap which courses through the trees carried the memories of the red man.

The white man's dead forget the country of their birth when they go to walk among the stars. Our dead never forget this beautiful earth, for it is the mother of the red man.

We are part of the earth and it is part of us. The perfumed flowers are our sisters; the deer, the horse, the great eagle, these are our brothers.

The rocky crests, the juices in the meadows, the body heat of the pony, and man – all belong to the same family.

So, when the Great Chief in Washington sends word that he wishes to buy our land, he asks much of us. The Great Chief sends word he will reserve us a place so that we can live comfortably to ourselves.

He will be our father and we will be his children. So we will consider your offer to buy our land.

But it will not be easy. For this land is sacred to us.

This shining water that moves in the streams and rivers is not just water but the blood of our ancestors.

If we sell you land, you must remember that it is sacred, and you must teach your children that it is sacred and that each ghostly reflection in the clear water of the lakes tells of events and memories in the life of my people.

The water's murmur is the voice of my father's father.

The rivers are our brothers, they quench our thirst. The rivers carry our canoes, and feed our children. If we sell you our land, you must remember, and teach your children, that the rivers are our brothers, and yours, and you must henceforth give the rivers the kindness you would give any brother.

We know that the white man does not understand our ways. One portion of land is the same to him as the next, for he is a stranger who comes in the night and takes from the land whatever he needs.

The earth is not his brother, but his enemy, and when he has conquered it, he moves on.

He leaves his father's graves behind, and he does not care. He kidnaps the earth from his children, and he does not care.

His father's grave and his children's birthright, are forgotten. He treats his mother, the earth, and his brother, the sky, as things to be bought, plundered, sold like sheep or bright beads.

His appetite will devour the earth and leave behind only a desert.

I do not know. Our ways are different from your ways.

The sight of your cities pains the eyes of the red man. But perhaps it is because the red man is a savage and does not understand.

There is no quiet place in the white man's cities. No place to hear the unfurling of leaves in spring, or the rustle of an insect's wings.

The clatter only seems to insult the ears. And what is there to life if a man cannot hear the lonely cry of the whippoorwill or the arguments of the frogs around a pond at night? I am a red man and do not understand.

The Indian prefers the soft sound of the wind darting over the face of a pond, and the smell of the wind itself, cleaned by a midday rain, or scented with the pinon pine.

The air is precious to the red man, for all things share the same breath – the beast, the tree, the man, they all share the same breath.

The white man does not seem to notice the air he breathes. Like a man dying for many days, he is numb to the stench.

But if we sell you our land, you must remember that the air is precious to us, that the air shares its spirit with all the life it supports. The wind that gave our grandfather his first breath also received his last sigh.

And if we sell you our land, you must keep it apart and sacred, as a place where even the white man can go to taste the wind that is sweetened by the meadow's flowers.

So we will consider your offer to buy our land. If we decide to accept, I will make one condition: the white man must treat the beasts of this land as his brother.

I am a savage and I do not understand any other way.

I have seen a thousand rotting buffaloes on the prairie, left by the white man who shot them from a passing train.

I am a savage and I do not understand how the smoking iron horse can be more important than the buffalo that we kill only to stay alive.

What is man without the beasts? If all the beasts were gone, man would die from a great loneliness of spirit.

For whatever happens to the beasts, soon happens to man. All things are connected.

You must teach your children that the ground beneath their feet is the ashes of your grandfathers. So that they will respect the land, tell your children that the earth is rich with the lives of our kin.

Teach your children what we have taught our children, that the earth is our mother.

Whatever befalls the earth befalls the sons of the earth. If men spit upon the ground, they spit upon themselves.

This we know: the earth does not belong to man; man belongs to the earth. This we know.

All things are connected like the blood which unites one family. All things are connected.

Whatever befalls the earth befalls the sons of the earth. Man did not weave the web of life: he is merely a strand in it. Whatever he does to the web, he does to himself.

Even the white man, whose God walks and talks with him as friend to friend, cannot be exempt from the common destiny.

We may be brothers after all.

We shall see.

One thing we know, which the white man may one day discover – our God is the same God.

You may think now that you own Him as you wish to own our land; but you cannot. He is the God of man, and His compassion is equal for the red man and the white.

This earth is precious to Him, and to harm the earth is to heap contempt on its Creator.

The whites too shall pass; perhaps sooner than all other tribes.

Contaminate your bed, and you will one night suffocate in your own waste.

AFTER READING

1 Why does the idea of selling the land seem 'strange' to Chief Seattle?

2 What emotions does this letter arouse in you? Discuss these with a partner and with other readers.

■ Mary Church Terrell was a leader in the fight against discrimination of African Americans, and was a founder of the National Association for the Advancement of Coloured People.

But in your perishing you will shine brightly, fired by the strength of the God who brought you to this land and for some special purpose gave you dominion over this and over the red man.

That destiny is a mystery to us, for we do not understand when the buffalo are all slaughtered, the wild horses are tamed, the secret corners of the forest heavy with scent of many men, and the view of the ripe hill blotted by talking wires.

> Where is the thicket? Gone
> Where is the eagle? Gone
> The end of living and the beginning of survival.

•••••

Mary Church Terrell to the editor of the Washington Post, 14 May 1949

Dear Sir:

Please stop using the word "Negro". Several days ago "BAN ON WORD ASKED" was the *Post*'s title of an appeal made by a leper who stood before a congressional committee urging that the Federal Government ban the use of the word "leper". He said the word "leper" should be removed from the dictionary because of its unjust and shameful stigma which hurts its victims, and efforts to control and wipe the disease out. He wants the affliction to be called "Hanson's Disease", because lepers are treated unfairly owing to "public misunderstanding".

For a reason similar to the one given by the leper I am urging the *Post* and others willing to advance our interests and deal justly with our group to stop using the word "Negro". The word is a misnomer from every point of view. It does not represent a country or anything else except one single, solitary colour. And no one colour can describe the various and varied complexions in our group. In complexion we range from deep black to the fairest white with all the colours of the rainbow thrown in for good measure. When twenty or thirty of us are meeting together it would be as hard to find three or four of us with the same complexion as it would be to catch greased lightning in a bottle. We are the only human beings in the world with fifty-seven varieties of complexions who are classed together as a single racial unit. Therefore, we are really, truly coloured people, and that is the only name in the English language which accurately describes us.

...When I studied abroad and was introduced as an "American" (generally speaking, everybody from the United States used to be called an "American" in Europe) occasionally somebody would say, "You are rather dark to be an American, aren't you?" "Yes," I would reply, "I am dark, because some of my ancestors were Africans." I was proud of having the continent of Africa part of my ancestral background. "I am an African-American", I would explain. I am not ashamed of my African descent. Africa had great universities before there were any in England and the African was the first man industrious and skillful enough to work in iron. If our group must have a special name setting it apart, the sensible way to settle it would be to refer to our ancestors, the Africans, from whom our swarthy complexions come.

There are at least two strong reasons why I object to designating our group as Negroes. If a man is a Negro, it follows as the night the day that a woman is a Negress. "Negress" is an ugly, repulsive word – virtually a term of degradation and reproach which coloured women of this country can not live down in a thousand years. I have questioned scores of men who call themselves "Negroes", and each and every one of them strenuously objected to having his wife, or daughter or mother or any woman in his family called a "Negress".

In the second place, I object to...Negro because our meanest detractors and most cruel persecutors insist that we shall be called by that name, so that they can humiliate us by referring contemptuously to us as "niggers", or "Negras" as Bilbo used to do. Some of our group say they will continue to classify us as Negroes, until an individual referred to as such will be proud of that name. But that is a case of wishful thinking and nothing else. For the moment one hears the word Negro in this country, instantly, automatically, in his mind's eye he sees a human being who is ignorant, segregated, discriminated against, considered inferior and objectionable on general principles from every point of view. God alone knows how long it will take our minority group under prevailing conditions in this country to reach such heights that a representative of it will be proud to be called a Negro. That would be a double, back action, super-duper miracle indeed!...

It is a great pity the word "Negro" was not outlawed in the Emancipation Proclamation as it certainly should have been. After people have been freed, it is a cruel injustice to call them by the same name they bore as slaves.

AFTER READING

1 What impression do you get of the character of Mary Church Terrell from reading this letter?

2 What impression do you get of life in the United States of America in 1949?

COMPARE

Discussion

1 Discuss in pairs what you think the main point is that the writer of each letter wants to make.

2 What do you learn about the lives and the hopes of Native Americans and African Americans from reading these letters? Discuss the differences and similarities between these two peoples (where they came from, how they were treated, etc).

Assignments

1 'If men spit upon the ground, they spit upon themselves' – Chief Seattle uses proverbs to warn the President of the dangers of mistreating the land. In pairs, find a few of these proverbs and discuss what they mean. Are Chief Seattle's warnings relevant for today's world? How relevant are the issues that Mary Church Terrell raises?

Now write your own proverb about something that you feel is important.

2 Neither letter writer had the power to implement their beliefs. Yet both of their letters contain a sense of authority and demand the respect and the careful attention of the reader. Write an essay examining the ways in which the writers achieve this. Consider the following points:

- What impact does each letter's opening sentence have?
- What evidence do the writers use to support the points they make?
- What key words are repeated throughout the letters, and what effect do they have?
- How powerful is the ending of each letter?

3 Write a letter in reply to either of the two letters. You could sympathise with the writer's view, or offer advice, or disagree. You could write the letter that the President of the United States might have written to Chief Seattle, or that a reader of the Washington Post (black or white) might have written in reply to Mary Church Terrell's letter.

WIDER READING

Letters in Fiction
Many writers use letters to further the plot of their novel, and to reveal secrets, see: Sue Townsend, *The Secret Diary of Adrian Mole*; Jane Austen, *Pride and Prejudice*; Jean Webster, *Daddy Long Legs*; Alice Walker, *The Colour Purple*.

Books of Letters
For examples of letters that were actually written see: *The Faber Book of Letters* (ed. Felix Pryor); *Welcome to Hell* (ed. Jan Arriens) – a collection of letters written by prisoners on death row in America.

AFTER READING

1 From your reading, write about two of the letters which have had a strong effect on you and why.

2 Write a letter to someone! It could be a formal letter, a personal letter to someone that you haven't seen for a while, a letter to a newspaper, etc.

FUTURES

Human beings have many different thoughts and feelings about the future. Sometimes we think about the future with excitement; at other times we fear what might happen to the world.
- *Who has most influence over your future?*
- *What future is there for life on earth?*

PARENTAL PRESSURE

■ How much control do young people have over their futures? What might stand in the way of them achieving their ambitions? The following three texts deal with children whose parents have certain expectations of them.

In the first, Adah, an eleven-year-old Nigerian girl, is adopted by her uncle's family when her father dies.

SECOND CLASS CITIZEN

Time went by quickly, and when she reached the age of eleven, people started asking her when she was going to leave school. This was an urgent question because the fund for Boy's education was running low; Ma was not happy with her new husband and it was considered time that Adah started making a financial contribution to her family. This terrified Adah. For a time it seemed as if she must give in to save Ma from the humiliating position she found herself in. She hated Ma for marrying again, thinking it was a betrayal of Pa. Sometimes she dreamt of marrying early; a rich man who would allow Ma and Boy to come and stay with her. That would have solved a lot of problems, but the kind of men that she was being pushed to by her clever cousins and Ma's tactful hints were bald and huge, almost as big as her dead Pa. Ma had told her that older men took better care of their wives than the young and overeducated ones, but Adah didn't like them. She would never, never in her life get married to any man, rich or poor, to whom she would have to serve his food on bended knee: she would not consent to live with a husband whom she would have to treat as a master and refer to as "Sir" even behind his back. She knew that all Ibo women did this, but she wasn't going to!

Unfortunately, her obstinacy gained her a very bad reputation; what nobody told her then was that the older men were encouraged to come and "talk" to her because only they could afford the high "bride-price" Ma was asking. Since, however, she didn't know this, as soon as she saw one of those "baldies" in his white starched trousers, she would burst into native songs about bad old baldies. If that failed to repel them, she would go to the back yard and burst the bicycle tyres of the suitors. She discovered later this was very bad indeed, because she had since learnt that the Nigerian Government usually gave the junior clerks an advance for these bicycles. All the suitors were doing then was to ask for the advance for their new Raleigh bikes with flashy lights in order to impress Adah. But the stupid girl refused to be impressed.

The number of suitors did start to dwindle, though. Maybe word went round that she was a peculiar girl, for she did look funny in those days; all head, with odd-coloured hair and a tummy that would have graced any Oxfam poster. She was subsequently told that they stopped coming because she was cranky and ugly. She did not dispute that; she was ugly then, all skin and bone.

The thought of her having to leave school at the end of the year worried her so much that she lost weight. She acquired a pathetically anxious look; the type some insane people have, with eyes as blank as contact lenses.

At about this time, something happened that showed her that her dream was just suffering a tiny dent, just a small one, nothing deep enough to destroy the basic structure. The dream had by now assumed an image in her mind, it seemed to take life, to breathe and to smile kindly at her. The smile of the Presence became wide as the headmaster of Adah's school announced the lists of available secondary schools which the children could apply for.

"You are going, you must go and to one of the very best of schools; not only are you going, you're going to do well there," Adah heard the Presence telling her. She heard it so much that she started to smile. The headmaster's voice jolted her back to reality.

"And what is it about me that you find so funny, Adah Ofili?"

"Me, sir? Oh, no, sir, I was not laughing, I mean not smiling, sir."

"You were not what? You mean I am lying? Well, back her up!"

Immediately a group of three or four tough-looking boys came out from the back row and the biggest of them all swept Adah onto his back and two others held her feet while the headmaster administered the cane on her posterior. The searing of the cane was so intense that Adah was beyond screaming. To ease the pain, she sank her sharp teeth deep into the back of the poor boy who was backing her. He started to scream loudly, but Adah would not let go, not even when the caning stopped. The boy wriggled in agony and so did Adah. All the teachers came to the rescue. Adah's teeth had dug so deep into him that fragments of his flesh were stuck between her teeth. She quickly spat them out and wiped her mouth, looking at them all wide-eyed.

"You'll go to jail for this," the headmaster thundered and he took the boy into his office for first aid. From that day on, no boy ever volunteered to back Adah any more, but that incident gave her a nickname which she never lived down: the Ibo tigress. Some of her Yoruba classmates used to ask her what human flesh tasted like, because "You Ibos used to eat people, didn't you?" Well, Adah didn't know about the cannibalistic tendencies of her tribe; all she knew was that the headmaster's cane burnt her so much that she felt irrepressible urges to pass the pain to something else. Latifu, the boy who was doing the backing, happened to be the closest victim, so he had to take it. Adah also felt that she was being unjustly punished. She had been smiling at the Presence, not the headmaster, and she suspected that the headmaster knew she was telling the truth; he had simply wanted to cane her, that was all.

Adah waited for days for the Law which the headmaster said was coming to take her to jail. No policeman came for her, so she decided that she had either been forgotten or that her bite of Latifu was not deep enough to merit imprisonment. The thought nagged her, though. It nagged her so much that she was tempted to commit another atrocity, this time a really horrible one that nearly sent her, not to jail, but to her Maker.

Adah was given two shillings to buy a pound of steak from a market called Sand Ground. She looked at the two-shilling piece for a very, very long time. All she needed to take the entrance examination to the school of her dreams was two shillings. Didn't Jesus say that one should not steal? But she was sure there was a place in the Bible where it said that one could be as clever as the serpent but as harmless as the dove. Would she be harming anybody if she paid for her entrance examination fee with this two shillings? Would Jesus condemn her for doing it: for stealing? After all, her cousin could afford the money, though he would not give it to her if she asked for it in the proper way. What was she to do? That was the trouble with Jesus, He never answered you; He never really gave you a sign of what to do in such a tempting situation. Anybody could twist what He said to suit his own interpretation. Then she saw the Image again. It was going to be all right, the Image was smiling, so Adah buried the money and went back home in tears, without the meat.

She was really no good at lying. The wildness in her eyes had a way of betraying her. If only she could have kept her large eyes lowered it would have been all right: people would have believed her story. But she kept staring into their eyes, and her face showed her up like a mirror.

"You're lying, Adah," her cousin's wife said, pointedly.

Adah opened her mouth, but had to close it quickly, because no sound came. She knew what was going to happen to her; the cane. She did not mind this caning because she knew that anybody who sinned must be punished. What she did not bargain for was the extent of the punishment. Her cousin sent her out with a three-penny piece to buy the type of cane called the *koboko*. It was the one the Hausas used for their horses. There was nothing Adah could do but buy it. Her cousin warned her that he would not stop administering the cane until she'd told him the truth. That was bad, thought Adah. She had to go to the Methodist Girls' High School or die. She concentrated her mind on something else. After the burning of the first few strokes, her skin became hardened, and so did her heart. She started to count. When Cousin Vincent had counted to fifty, he appealed to Adah to cry a little. If only she would cry and beg for mercy, he would let her go. But Adah would not take the bait. She began to see herself as another martyr; she was being punished for what she believed in. Meanwhile Cousin Vincent's anger increased; he caned her wildly, all over her body. After a hundred and three strokes, he told Adah that he would never talk to her again: not in this world nor in the world to come. Adah did not mind that. She was, in fact, very happy. She had earned the two shillings.

The headmaster at her school did not believe his ears when Adah told him that she was going to sit for the common entrance examination. He looked at her kwashiorkor-ridden body for a very long time then shrugged his shoulders. "One can never tell with you Ibos. You're the greatest mystery the good God has created." So he put her name down.

Sometimes the thought that she might not be able to pay the fees crossed her mind. But she did not let that worry her. She had read somewhere that there was some sort of scholarship for the five or so children who did best in the exam. She was going to compete for one of these places. She was so determined that not even the fact that her number was nine hundred and forty-seven frightened her. She was going to that school, and that was that!

But how was she to tell them at home? She had stopped liking Cousin Vincent. Every time she knelt down to pray, she used to tell God to send him to hell. She did not believe in that stuff of loving your enemy. After all, God did not like the Devil, so why should she pray for the man who had the heart to cane her for a good two hours with a *koboko*? When Cousin Vincent failed his Cambridge School Certificate examinations, Adah burst out laughing. God had heard her prayers.

The entrance examination was to take place on a Saturday. That was going to be very difficult. How was she to get away? Another lie? She could not do that again. She would be discovered, and they would stop her from taking the examination; so she told her uncle, Ma's brother, that she was going to sit for the examination. The funniest thing was that nobody even asked her where she got the money from. Nobody wanted to know. As long as she was not asking for money from anybody, and as long as she had done her Saturday job, she could go to the devil for all they cared!

Occasionally, the mother of the house, Ma's sister-in-law, would ask how she proposed to get the money for the school fees and remind her that her father was dead. In response, Adah's mind would flutter with fear, but she never told anyone she was dreaming of winning a scholarship. That was too big an ambition for a girl like her to express.

She was aware that nobody was interested in her since Pa died. Even if she had failed, she would have accepted it as one of the hurdles of life. But she did not fail. She not only passed the entrance examination. But she got a scholarship with full board. She never knew whether she came first or second or even third, but she was one of the best children that year.

Since then she had started to be overawed by the Presence. It existed right beside her, just like a companion. It comforted her during the long school holidays when she could not go home, because there was no home for her to go to.

BUCHI EMECHETA

1 Adah is guided by a 'presence' and an 'image'. In pairs, define what these words mean and what effect they have on Adah.

2 List the hurdles Adah has to overcome in order to go to High School.

■ Two girls from similar backgrounds end up with very different lives.

The Choosing

We were first equal Mary and I
with the same coloured ribbons in mouse-coloured hair,
and with equal shyness
we curtsied to the lady councillor
for copies of Collins Children's Classics.
First equal, equally proud.

Best friends too Mary and I
a common bond in being cleverest (equal)
in our small school's small class.
I remember
the competition for top desk
or to read aloud the lesson
at school service.
And my terrible fear
of her superiority at sums.

I remember the housing scheme
Where we both stayed.
The same house, different homes,
where the choices were made.

I don't know exactly why they moved,
but anyway they went.
Something about a three-apartment
and a cheaper rent.
But from the top deck of the high-school bus
I'd glimpse among the others on the corner
Mary's father, mufflered, contrasting strangely
with the elegant greyhounds by his side.

He didn't believe in high-school education,
especially for girls,
or in forking out for uniforms.

Ten years later on a Saturday –
I am coming home from the library –
sitting near me on the bus,
Mary
with a husband who is tall,
curly haired, has eyes
for no one else but Mary.
Her arms are round the full-shaped vase
that is her body.
Oh, you can see where the attraction lies
in Mary's life –
not that I envy her, really.

And I am coming from the library
with my arms full of books.
I think of the prizes that were ours for the taking
and wonder when the choices got made
we don't remember making.

LIZ LOCHHEAD

AFTER READING

1 Who made the choices for Liz (the author) and for Mary?

2 What effect did the choices have on Liz's and Mary's lives?

■ Written over one
hundred years ago, this
novel by Elizabeth Gaskell
tells of life in a small town
in Victorian times. Here,
an old woman, Miss
Matty, is recalling her
childhood. She remembers
her older sister Deborah
and her brother Peter, who
she has not seen since he
left home in disgrace after
this incident.

Cranford

Poor Peter's career lay before him rather pleasantly mapped out by kind friends, but *Bonus Bernardus non videt omnia*, in this map too. He was to win honours at Shrewsbury School, and carry them thick to Cambridge, and after that, a living awaited him, the gift of his godfather, Sir Peter Arley. Poor Peter! his lot in life was very different to what his friends had hoped and planned. Miss Matty told me all about it, and I think it was a relief to her when she had done so.

He was the darling of his mother, who seemed to dote on all her children, though she was, perhaps, a little afraid of Deborah's superior acquirements. Deborah was the favourite of her father, and when Peter disappointed him, she became his pride. The sole honour Peter brought away from Shrewsbury, was the reputation of being the best good fellow that ever was, and of being the captain of the school in the art of practical joking. His father was disappointed, but set about remedying the matter in a manly way. He could not afford to send Peter to read with any tutor, but he could read with him himself; and Miss Matty told me much of the awful preparations in the way of dictionaries and lexicons that were made in her father's study the morning Peter began.

'My poor mother!' said she. 'I remember how she used to stand in the hall, just near enough the study-door to catch the tone of my father's voice. I could tell in a moment if all was going right, by her face. And it did go right for a long time.'

'What went wrong at last?' said I. 'That tiresome Latin, I dare say.'

'No! it was not the Latin. Peter was in high favour with my father, for he worked up well for him. But he seemed to think that the Cranford people might be joked about, and made fun of, and they did not like it; nobody does. He was always hoaxing them; "hoaxing" is not a pretty word, my dear, and I hope you won't tell your father I used it, for I should not like him to think that I was not choice in my language, after living with such a woman as Deborah. And be sure you never use it yourself. I don't know how it slipped out of my mouth, except it was that I was thinking of poor Peter, and it was always his expression. But he was a very gentlemanly boy in many things. He was like dear Captain Brown in always being ready to help any old person or a child. Still, he did like joking and making fun; and he seemed to think the old ladies in Cranford would believe anything. There were many old ladies living here then; we are principally ladies now, I know; but we are not so old as the ladies used to be when I was a girl. I could laugh to think of some of Peter's jokes....

He used to say, the old ladies in the town wanted something to talk about; but I don't think they did. They had the St. James's Chronicle three times a-week, just as we have now, and we have plenty to say; and I remember the clacking noise there always was when some of the ladies got together. But, probably, school-boys talk more than ladies. At last there was a terrible sad thing happened.' Miss Matty got up, went to the door, and opened it; no one was there. She rang the bell for Martha; and when Martha came, her mistress told her to go for eggs to a farm at the other end of the town.

'I will lock the door after you, Martha. You are not afraid to go, are you?

'No, Ma'am, not at all; Jem Hearn will be only too proud to go with me.'

Miss Matty drew herself up, and, as soon as we were alone, she wished that Martha had more maidenly reserve.

'We'll put out the candle, my dear. We can talk just as well by fire-light, you know. There! well! you see, Deborah had gone from home for a fortnight or so; it was a very still, quiet day, I remember, overhead; and the lilacs were all in flower, so I suppose it was spring. My father had gone out to see some sick people in the parish; I recollect seeing him leave the house, with his wig and shovel-hat, and cane. What possessed our poor Peter I don't know; he had the sweetest temper, and yet he always seemed to like to plague Deborah. She never laughed at his jokes, and thought him ungenteel, and not careful enough about improving his mind; and that vexed him.

'Well! he went to her room, it seems, and dressed himself in her old gown, and shawl, and bonnet; just the things she used to wear in Cranford, and was known by everywhere; and he made the pillow into a little – you are sure you locked the door, my dear, for I should not like anyone to hear – into – into – a little baby with white long clothes. It was only, as he told me afterwards, to make something to talk about in the town: he never thought of it as affecting Deborah. And he went and walked up and down in the Filbert walk – just half hidden by the rails, and half seen; and he cuddled his pillow, just like a baby; and talked to it all the nonsense people do. Oh dear! and my father came stepping stately up the street, as he always did; and what should he see but a little black crowd of people – I dare say as many as twenty – all peeping through his garden rails. So he thought, at first, they were only looking at a new rhododendron that was in full bloom, and that he was very proud of; and he walked slower, that they might have more time to admire. And he wondered if he could make out a sermon from the occasion, and thought, perhaps, there was some relation between the rhododendrons and the lilies of the field. My poor father! When he came nearer, he began to wonder that they did not see him; but their heads were all so close together, peeping and peeping! My father was amongst them, meaning, he said, to ask them to walk into the garden with him, and admire the beautiful vegetable production, when – oh, my dear! I tremble to think of it – he looked through the rails himself, and saw – I don't know what he thought he saw, but old Clare told me his face went quite grey-white with anger, and his eyes blazed out under his frowning black brows; and he spoke out oh, so terribly! – and bade them all stop where they were – not one of them to go, and not one to stir a step; and, swift as light, he was in at the garden door, and down the Filbert walk, and seized hold of poor Peter, and tore his clothes off his back – bonnet, shawl, gown, and all – and threw the pillow among the people over the railings: and then he was very, very angry indeed; and before all the people he lifted up his cane, and flogged Peter!

'My dear! that boy's trick, on that sunny day, when all seemed going straight and well, broke my mother's heart, and changed my father for life. It did, indeed. Old Clare said, Peter looked as white as my father; and stood as still as a statue to be flogged; and my father struck hard! When my father stopped to take breath, Peter said, "Have you done enough, Sir?" quite hoarsely, and still standing quite quiet. I don't know what my father said – or if he said anything. But old Clare said, Peter turned to where the people outside the railing were, and made them a low bow, as grand and as grave as any gentleman; and then walked slowly into the house. I was in the store-room helping my mother to make cowslip-wine. I cannot abide the wine now, nor the scent of the flowers; they turn me sick and faint, as they did that day, when Peter came in, looking as haughty as any man – indeed looking like a man, not like a boy. "Mother!" he said, "I am come to say, God bless you for ever." I saw his lips quiver as he spoke; and I think he durst not say anything more loving, for the purpose that was in his heart. She looked at him rather frightened, and wondering, and asked him what was to do? He did not smile or speak, but put his arms round her, and kissed her as if he did not know how to leave off; and before she could speak again, he was gone. We talked it over, and could not understand it, and she bade me go and seek my father, and ask what it was all about. I found him walking up and down, looking very highly displeased.

"Tell your mother I have flogged Peter, and that he richly deserved it."

'I durst not ask any more questions. When I told my mother, she sat down, quite faint, for a minute. I remember, a few days after, I saw the poor, withered cowslip-flowers thrown out to the leaf-heap, to decay and die there. There was no making of cowslip-wine that year at the Rectory – nor, indeed, ever after.

ELIZABETH GASKELL

AFTER READING

1 What trick did Peter play and why did his father flog him for it?

2 Choose one word to describe Peter, one for Deborah and one for Matty.

COMPARE

Discussion

1 What are the main differences between the futures that Peter's parents planned for him, and the futures that were planned for Adah and Mary?

2 In pairs discuss how the personalities of Adah, Mary and Peter differ, and how they are similar. How does their behaviour affect their futures?

3 Cranford was written in Victorian times, when it was generally accepted that men would follow a career and that women would stay at home and raise a family. The poem, 'The Choosing', and the book, *Second Class Citizen*, were written very recently, yet both make the point that girls still do not have the same life chances as boys. What do you think? Is sexual discrimination in the home and in society a thing of the past, or is it still a real problem for many girls? Discuss this issue in pairs. Decide upon three points that you feel are important and share these with the rest of the class.

Assignments

1 In groups of four, work on a role play based on one of the following ideas:

* Adah is seen by the Headmaster after she has been whipped by her cousin. Worried about her appearance, he contacts the social services department. A social worker visits Adah's house to investigate what has happened. S/he interviews Adah, her mother, and her cousin Vincent. Discuss what each of these characters might have said when interviewed, then work out a scene to present to the rest of the class.

* You are Mary's teacher. You know that Mary has the ability to do well at school, and you are concerned that her father is limiting her future possibilities in life. You arrange an interview with Mary's father, her mother and Mary herself. Working in groups of four discuss what each character might have said at the interview, then work out a scene to present to the rest of the class.

2 What do you think happens next to Adah, Mary and Peter. Who has the most fulfilling life, and why? Write the next part of one of the stories.

3 Write a poem or an essay about your ambitions for your own future.

FACING THE FUTURE

■ Is there a future for life on earth? The following two extracts show two different views.

TURNING THE TIDE

There's certainly been no shortage of human development over the last thirty years. Scientists have challenged the very laws of nature, experimenting with genetics and bio-technology; technologists have taken humanity to the moon and sent machines to probe the solar system. We have hydro-electric and nuclear power, factory-farming and supersonic flight, wonder drugs, colour television, and the home computer.

With all the knowledge and skill behind these developments, no-one on earth need go cold or hungry; nobody need die in pain. Through transatlantic travel, and the media of international newsprint, signal, satellite, cable television and radio, we can observe the life-styles and customs of different countries at first hand. At the flick of a switch, nation can speak unto nation...and at least debate the insanities of another war. We have become residents of an international community, neighbours in a Global Village.

With these achievements we have the ability, the power, and clearly the energy and commitment to do immeasurable good. But it's all been too one-sided. The other side of progress doesn't look so good – the resource losses and environmental damage which have occurred in those thirty years have the combined potential to bring the 20th-century technological revolution and the complete human and planetary evolution to a sudden and nasty end. The check-list is dangerous and frightening. On the Doomsday Clock, it is a countdown to disaster:

TEN... A third of the world's human population is on the verge of starvation. 28 children under 5 years die every minute from conditions relating to malnutrition and environmental pollution.

NINE...   A third of the world's arable land surface is turning into a desert due to human misuse. The world is losing an average of 8 tonnes of soil per hectare per year – but the maximum rate of soil replenishment is less than 5 tonnes per hectare per year, and nearly 21 million hectares of good land have been reduced to a state of agricultural uselessness.

EIGHT...   World fisheries have declined drastically since 1970 as a result of over-fishing. There has been no real attempt to conserve stocks and species.

SEVEN...   Our over-dependence on genetically uniform mega-crops of maize, rice and wheat means that diseases can wipe out much of the crop, with catastrophic effects worldwide.

SIX...   World agricultural production has become over dependent on high energy inputs and on all kinds of fragile and wavering supports and subsidies: a precarious oil, chemical and capital fix.

FIVE...   The world's population is out of hand. It has risen from 1000 million in the 1800s to 2526 million in 1950 and 4433 million in 1980. In less than forty years it will have nearly doubled again. And where are the resources to cope?

FOUR...   We have already consumed more than half of the world's total reserves of coal, oil and natural gas which have fuelled the past 250 years of our success – and took around 300 million years to form. The resources which remain are less accessible and require more precious energy to extract.

THREE... Atomic power is now realized *not* to be the safe source of cheap, unlimited energy we were once told it would be.

TWO...   What's left of the world's great tropical rainforests, now covering less than 6% of the earth's surface, are being destroyed. Since 1950, Latin America has lost 35%, Central America 66%, South-East Asia 38% and Central Africa 52%. These are the world's greatest genetic banks, containing nearly half of all known plant and animal species, and they've been broken into.

ONE...   We have enough armaments to blow up the world many times over, and the stock-piles are still growing, increasing the ever-present risk of nuclear disaster by accident. We are now even talking about introducing nuclear and anti-nuclear weapons systems into space, the star wars dream, of the munitions-mungers and the 'defence' scientists.

ZERO...   BANG! Put that lot together, throw in even a 'limited' thermo-nuclear war and there will be nothing left to say and no-one left to say it. Life on earth , if it survives at all, would be a sorry, sickly, poisoned thing.

DAVID BELLAMY & BRENDAN QUAYLE

AFTER READING

1 Working in pairs, write out a definition of the following terms by examining the ways the words are used in the passage. Then compare your definitions of these terms with those in a dictionary. Were you correct?
- Genetics
- Bio Technology
- Supersonic
- Solar System
- Hydro Electric
- Nuclear.

■ This extract is taken from a B&Q newspaper advertisement. It suggests that we can help the environment in many different ways.

The more we look into environmental issues, the more environmental issues we find to look into

ALL PRODUCTS HAVE AN IMPACT.

People, business and retailers all have an impact on the environment.

As a retailer our most significant impact is caused by the products we sell. We are committed to reducing that impact.

WE HAVE A RESPONSIBILITY.

However, the impact does not occur when the product sits on our stores' shelves but at other stages in its long and complex life cycle – from the cradle to the grave.

Despite that, our first step on the ladder to environmental improvement was to acknowledge that we have a responsibility to reduce that impact wherever feasible.

This basic principle is the heart of our environmental policy. But it is a responsibility that we must share with all the other links in the supply chain. At the same time, we must reduce our impact in store and in our other operations.

THE LIFE CYCLE OF A PRODUCT.

'Even a hammer has an impact'.

Who would have considered that a hammer could have a significant environmental impact?

Yet the timber shaft comes from a forest and the metal head originally comes from a quarry. To turn that wood and metal ore into a hammer requires manufacturing which uses up energy and creates waste. When the hammer is broken can it be repaired or recycled?

Another example is car engine oil; we can strive to ensure that it is made in environmentally safer ways but if it is disposed of in a country ditch it will still be polluting.

TIMBER

The extraction of timber, along with many other factors, contributes to the destruction of the world's natural forests.

However, a society that uses no timber is unimaginable – but if it produced truly sustainable timber, then timber would arguably be one of the most environmentally acceptable raw materials available to us.

B&Q supports the work of organisations and individuals across the world who are working to establish detailed principles and criteria for good forest management. These principles need to be applicable to all the world's timber and should include detailed criteria on social issues and species protection.

B&Q's TARGET

BY THE END OF 1993 B&Q WILL NOT PURCHASE ANY TIMBER FROM AN UNKNOWN SOURCE.

B&Q's TARGET

BY THE END OF 1995 IF WE ARE NOT SATISFIED WOOD COMES FROM A WELL-MANAGED SOURCE, WE WILL NOT BUY IT.

AFTER READING

1 This extract comes from a four-page newspaper advertisement and must have cost a great deal to place in a national newspaper. In pairs, discuss why B&Q decided to publish it.

2 List what you think are the most important points this extract makes.

COMPARE

Discussion

1 The two passages are designed to affect you, the reader, in different ways. Choose one of the following words that would best describe your feelings after reading *Turning the Tide,* and after reading the B&Q advertisement: shocked, upset, reassured, optimistic, pessimistic, angry, hopeful. Which passage argued its points more succesfully?

2 Point two of *Turning the Tide* details the threat to the world's tropical rainforests. In pairs, discuss and list what B&Q is doing to safeguard the world's rainforests. Is it enough?

Assignments

1 Find out as much as you can about the threat to the environment. You may find useful information in libraries, from campaign leaflets for environmental groups such as Friends of the Earth or Greenpeace. Use the information that you have collected to write an essay on the subject that you have investigated. Be careful not to copy large passages from the texts that you have read. Rather, use the information to back up the points that you want to make. Design an effective front cover for your essay.

2 Look again at the Doomsday Clock in *Turning the Tide*. For each of the ten points, write an answering statement saying what you would do to solve the problem. Keep your style short and direct. Write up your statements on a poster and present it in a way that would catch the eye.

3 Design an advertisement about one of the problems facing the world. Your advert is aimed at increasing public awareness of this problem and suggesting ways in which people can act to help the situation.

WIDER READING

Science-fiction novels
Nicholas Fisk, *Grinny* and *Robot Revenge*; H G Wells, *War of the Worlds*; Harry Harrison, *The Stainless Steel Rat*; Ursula Le Guin, *The Word For World Is Forest*; John Wyndham, *The Midwich Cuckoos*; Terry Pratchett, *The Colour of Magic*; Jules Verne, *Journey To The Centre Of The Earth.*

AFTER READING

1 Compare two of the science fiction stories that you have read saying what warnings that they give us about human society.

2 Write a personal essay describing the appeal of science fiction stories.

Acknowledgments

We should like to thank the following authors and publishers for permission to reproduce copyright material:

John Murray (Publishers) Ltd, extract from 'Beside the Seaside' by John Betjeman, p.3; extract from *Five on Finniston Farm* by Enid Blyton, © Darrell Waters Ltd 1960, p.5; Laura Gladwin, book review, p.8; extract from *A Welsh Childhood* by Alice Thomas Ellis (Michael Joseph, 1990) copyright © Alice Thomas Ellis, 1990, reproduced by permission of Michael Joseph Ltd, p.14; extract from *Great Meadow* by Dirk Bogarde (Viking, 1992) copyright © Motley Films Ltd, reproduced by permission of Penguin Books, p.18; Richard Scott Simon Ltd, 'Sing-Song Time' from *George, Don't Do That* © Joyce Grenfell 1977, p.22; Ward Lock Educational, 'Living Cloud' by Stephen Bell, published in *Into Poetry*, ed Richard Andrews, p.27; extract from *The Nature of the Beast* © Janni Howker, permission granted by the publishers Walker Books Ltd, p.28; Rupert Hart-Davies (an imprint of HarperCollins Publishers), extract from *My Family and Other Animals* by Gerald Durrell, p.32; McDonald's Restaurants Ltd, 'Did You Know' fact sheet, p.39; Dr John Collee, 'Animal Crackers' first published by the *Observer* in the series 'A Doctor Writes', p.40; The British Union for the Abolition of Vivisection, publicity leaflet, p.42; Kingfisher Books, 'Pandora's Box' from *The Kingfisher Book of Myths and Legends* by Anthony Horowitz, copyright © Grisewood and Dempsey, p.45; The University of Chicago Press, 'The Midwife and the Frog' from *Folk Tales of Hungary*, p.55; 'Rabbit in Mixer Survives' from *Selected Poems 1967-87* by Roger McGough, published by Jonathan Cape, reprinted by permission of the Peters, Fraser & Dunlop Group Ltd, p.62; Samuel Selvon, extract from *A Brighter Sun*, published by the Longman Group, p.67; 'The Happiest Days of My Life' (abridged), © The *Guardian*, p.68; Indiana University Press, 'Ain't I a Woman?' by Erlene Stetson, adapted from the speech by Sojourner Truth from *Black Sister: Poetry by Black American Women*, p.76; Martin Luther King, 'I Have a Dream', p.77; *The Unexplained – Mysteries of Mind, Space and Time*, 'Are You Psychically Aware?', p.80; 'Sasquatch Sightings' adapted from *On the Track of the Sasquatch* and *The Sasquatch File* by John Green, published by Cheam Publishing Ltd, and in *Mysteries of the Unexplained* by Reader's Digest, p.83; Tim Crawley, 'Put Your Best Bigfoot Forward', p.85; Robinson Publishing, 'The Inhabited Universe' from *The Giant Book of the Unknown*, ed Colin Wilson and Christopher Evans, p.88; Weekly World News Inc, 'Starship Lands in Wheatfield', p.91; Xanadu Publications Ltd, 'The Look of Death' by Jean Cocteau, p.93, and 'Ending for a Ghost Story' by IA Ireland, p.94, both published in *The Book of Fantasy*, ed Borges, Octampo, Casares; Rudolph Kizerman, 'Edication', published by Thomas Nelson in *Standpoints*, ed John Foster, p.100; *The Independent*, 'More Fat than Fit' by Steve Connor, p.112; Methuen Drama, extract from *The Golden Girls* by Louise Page, p.114; 'Miss Otis Regrets', words and music by Cole Porter © 1933 Harms Inc, USA, Warner Chappell Music Ltd, London, reproduced by permission of International Music Publications Ltd, p.118; Rupert Williams, 'The Miss Otis Case', p.119; extract from 'Handcarved Coffins' from *Music for Chameleons* by Truman Capote (Hamish Hamilton, 1981) copyright © Truman Capote, 1979, reproduced by permission of Hamish Hamilton Ltd, p.127; Crime statistics from *Hutchinson Gallop Info 1992*, published by Random Century, p.133; Mary Church Terrell, Letter to the Editor of the Washington Post, p.152; Dr Buchi Emecheta, extract from *Second Class Citizen*, published by Allison and Busby, p.156; Polygon, 'The Choosing' by Liz Lochhead, p.161; William Collins and Sons Ltd, extract from *Turning the Tide* by David Bellamy and Brendan Quayle, p.167; B&Q plc, extract from 'The More We Look into Environmental Issues...', p.169.

The authors and publishers would like to thank the following for permission to reproduce illustrations:

BUAV, p.42; The Dickens House Museum, London, p.66; Dover Books, pp 7, 9, 16, 26, 34, 41, 43, 45, 51, 52, 53, 55, 62, 63, 79, 118, 137, 141, 143, 146 and 150; Fortean Picture Library, pp 83, 88 and 92; Gay Galsworthy, pp 59 and 60; Hulton Deutsch, p.77; Gaynor Lloyd, p.4; McDonald's Restaurants Ltd, p.39; The Mansell Collection, pp 12, 103, 104, 105, 110 and 111; Panos Pictures, p.156; The Science Photo Library, p. 167, Turner Entertainment Co; All Rights Reserved © 1953, p.73, © 1941, p.120.

Although every effort has been made to contact the holders of copyright material, this has not been possible in every case. We apologise for any inadvertent infringement of copyright.